CRONE OF SOLSTICE FLAMES

IRIS BEAGLEHOLE

Iris Beaglehole

CHAPTER 1
DELIA

I t was a most excellent start to the morning. Delia had savoured a substantial full English breakfast at the Witch's Wort. She was fuelled up for the day, with an extra cup of coffee in her travel mug, as she drove the short distance to the address Sherry had provided. Given the proximity, she could have walked, though after such a hearty breakfast, it might have taken her some time.

The adorable row of terraced houses made her smile. The old brick buildings had neat little rose gardens out the front like something out of a fairy tale village.

Delia parked in front of number eight at the end of the row. She was about to get out of her car when she spotted a familiar handsome young man from the pub strolling along the street in her direction.

Wanting to avoid an awkward interaction, Delia decided to

stay in the car and just enjoy the view from afar. He hadn't caught her eye, so he probably hadn't noticed her, and she intended to keep it that way until he was safely past. However, rather than continuing down the street, he swung open the little white gate to the very house she intended to visit and began walking up the path.

Delia, for no apparent rational reason, felt a blaze of rage.

How dare he try and get the house that she wanted to rent? It was adorable and perfect for the grandchildren, especially if it had a big back garden. Sherry had said it backed onto a park, and she was sure it was good inside as well, to match the meticulously cared-for exterior. Houses for rent were notoriously hard to come by in Myrtlewood and Delia wasn't about to lose this one.

She got out of the car, slammed the door, and stormed out behind Liam.

"Excuse me," she said, trying to smile and also trying not to set anything on fire. "I was here first."

"Err...excuse me?" Liam looked at her with a puzzled expression. "Uhh...Good. Delia, is it?"

"That's right," she said, and there was a moment of hesitation.

They both looked around.

"So you're here to view the house then?" Liam asked.

"Yes, I have grandchildren, you see, and I need somewhere nice where they can come and visit. It's very important."

Liam smiled. "I wouldn't have thought you'd be old enough

to have grandchildren. You must have been a very young mother."

Delia glared at him. "Don't you try to charm me, young man. I'm old enough to be your mother, and you can't take this house out from underneath me. Sherry didn't tell me there was any competition for it. Now where is she? She doesn't seem like the sort to be running late."

"Ahh. Is that what you think is going on here?" He grinned at her and winked, then pulled a key out of his pocket and opened the door.

Delia buckled slightly in a wave of nauseating embarrassment. "Oh, you're not trying to rent the house?"

"It's my mother's house." Liam grinned.

"Oh," said Delia awkwardly. "So you and Sherry are..."

"Cousins."

"Good," said Delia, swallowing her embarrassment as Liam pushed the door open with his rather buff arms and gestured for her to enter.

"I hear it's hard to find a place to rent around here," he said, as if trying to explain away her abruptness from moments before.

"So I've been told," said Delia. "Thanks for showing me the place."

She walked in, immediately appreciating the hardwood floors, with barely any signs of wear. "Does it come furnished?" She looked around at the slightly mismatched décor and the Victorian, Edwardian, and other eras of furnishings.

"Mum doesn't need any of this stuff where she's going," Liam replied.

For a moment, Delia wanted to express her condolences. Then she recalled Sherry had said his mother had moved to Spain. "I suppose not," she said, happily avoiding another social faux pas.

The kitchen seemed fairly modern, putting it slightly at odds with the rest of the house, but it looked practical. There were two large bedrooms and an upstairs loft with twin beds, which would be perfect for the grandchildren.

"I'll take it," said Delia as she looked out on a gorgeous back garden with a vegetable patch, a decent-looking herb bed close to the back door, several fruit trees, and enough lawn for the kids to run around on. Merryn would be straight through the gate and into the park to climb trees. There was even a little gate at the back that led out to the park Sherry had spoken of. "It's perfect."

"I haven't told you how much it is yet," said Liam.

Delia shrugged. "If that lawyer in town is as good as my daughter says, it won't matter. Besides, once I cancel my lease in London, I won't have any other bills to pay."

"That lawyer..." said Liam with a stern note in his voice, looking concerned. "You're talking about Perseus Burk?"

"Yeah, I think that's his name," said Delia, looking through her handbag for her phone. She raised an eyebrow at Liam in the awkward silence. "From the tone of your voice, you sound like you don't like him very much. Should I be worried?"

"Definitely. I don't trust him as far as I could throw him. Then again, I have my reasons." Liam looked out towards the garden.

Delia pressed her lips together in a fine line, sensing some kind of territorial fight. "As long as none of them have to do with his legal practice, and he's not terribly dangerous, I think I'll be fine."

Liam cleared his throat. "Not to do with his legal practice," he said awkwardly, "but he is dangerous."

"Most people in this town are dangerous, it seems," Delia remarked.

Liam chuckled. "Fair point."

"I almost set you on fire before," Delia admitted.

Liam laughed, flashing his pearly whites at her. He seemed nice and normal, but who really knew around here.

It turned out the house was a very reasonable price, and Delia signed the lease before she even left the viewing. She didn't get the sense that Liam would be a terrible landlord, even if he was a bit of a flirt. He seemed harmless enough, although perhaps he was just as dangerous as everyone else in Myrtlewood.

CHAPTER 2
MARJIE

Marjie inhaled the sweet scent of cinnamon, revelling in the cosy environment of her bustling tea shop. The air was also heavy with the rich scent of freshly baked scones, each a buttery offering of comfort straight from the oven. She smiled and brewed a special blend of tea; the herby aroma of sage and camomile added an aura of mysticism.

The clinking of porcelain teacups and the murmur of satisfied customers created a symphony of everyday life, a sharp contrast to the arcane adventures she had been on recently.

She had been up since the crack of dawn, her fingers dancing deftly over a mixing bowl, her work humming with magical energies. Her creations weren't just scones, cakes, and pasties; they were little parcels of enchantment of a subtle nature, bursting with flavours to warm the heart.

Despite the frenetic pace of life she'd endured, galloping

through the countryside in the last few days to unleash spells woven from the most ancient threads of crone magic, Marjie felt invigorated.

There was a tingling sensation right at her fingertips, like the residual magic had somehow infused her very being, making her more alive, more vibrant than she had felt in years.

Just then, the bell above the door jingled melodiously.

"Marjie!" Papa Jack's warm and caring voice rang through the shop like a gentle summer breeze, clearing away any lingering clouds of worry.

She looked up and there he was, striding in with that winning smile of his – the kind that seemed to twinkle right from the depths of his clear blue eyes.

"Hello, my dear!" she exclaimed, her face lighting up as she hurried over to greet him.

Their hug was like sinking into an old, comfortable chair, soothing and reassuring.

He pulled away and looked at her, his gaze as soft as it was serious.

"I was quite worried about you, Marjie," he said, his voice tinged with a palpable concern that settled around her like an old blanket – comfortable, but his worry was slightly scratchy.

She averted her gaze, her mind rippling momentarily with the echoes of an intimate conversation they had shared at the pub.

That moment seemed a lifetime ago, even if it had been merely a day or two.

Time is a funny thing, she mused. *It behaves in exactly the way a serious thing ought not to. Time has the elasticity of dough under a skilled baker's hands – stretching and compressing in bewildering ways.*

"Oh, I'm fine," she assured him, forcing herself back to the present. "Nothing to trouble yourself over."

As she spoke, her eyes flitted towards the window and caught sight of Delia.

The slightly younger woman meandered down the cobblestone street, her path leading towards the apothecary. The sight triggered a new flurry of thoughts.

Delia, Agatha, Ingrid – they were becoming increasingly central to Marjie's life, along with the unfolding mysteries around them.

Ingrid's insistence that they had only scratched the surface of their powers sent a shiver snaking its way down Marjie's spine.

Papa Jack broke through her reverie. "Are you sure you're quite alright? You seem lost in thought."

Marjie shot him a reassuring smile. "Of course I am. I'm just thinking about my new friends. The usual tea?"

He nodded and she turned to prepare his favourite blend.

As she steeped the leaves, the rising steam seemed to whisper secrets, filling the room with a scent that was a blend of comfort and anticipation. For a moment, Marjie stood there, teapot in hand, and felt a reassuring certainty settle over her.

The tapestry of past, present, and future was still being

woven, and she, along with the Myrtlewood Crones, were the weavers of their own intricate, magical story.

Picking up a rose patterned teacup, Marjie poured the steaming liquid, watching as it swirled into the cup.

The scent was a comforting blend of earthiness and warmth, tinged with the slight bitterness that added strength. It was a blend she had perfected over the years, imbued with a hint of magic that gave it that extra kick – a taste of home, a kiss of nostalgia, a touch of the extraordinary.

Setting the cup and saucer before Papa Jack, she watched as he lifted it to his lips, sipping cautiously at first, then with evident satisfaction. "Ah, Marjie, you make tea as if you've charmed the leaves themselves," he commented, his eyes closing momentarily in sheer appreciation.

She chuckled, her eyes lighting up. "Who's to say I haven't?"

Their laughter mingled with the background chatter of other customers, settling into the air like an extra layer of warmth.

Marjie turned to the counter and began to clear it, her fingers lingering over a jar of her 'Winter's Embrace' tea blend.

"Is that the new one?" Papa Jack asked, reaching towards the jar.

"Oh yes," said Marjie.

"Ginger, clove, cinnamon, and orange peel..." Papa Jack read.

"That's right," Marjie said warmly. "The ginger brings a spicy zest that enlivens the senses, while the clove adds depth with its earthy, slightly sweet aroma. Cinnamon adds another note of familiar warmth—"

"It tastes exactly like Christmas – or Yule, I suppose," said Papa Jack. "Yule is a much bigger deal around here, I gather."

Marjie beamed at him. "Yes, of course. I wanted to make something uplifting and cosy."

"Well, you've succeeded. The orange peel adds a zest that cuts through the winter gloom," Papa Jack added. "Perfect for sipping during the long cold nights."

Marjie's thoughts drifted off into daydreams of winter nights snuggled by the fire with the wonderful kind man in front of her, before she pulled herself back to the present. Her husband, Herb, had only passed so recently. Besides, Papa Jack was a wonderful friend. She'd hate to lose him to an ill-conceived romantic tryst. She was far too sensible – and busy.

She went back to wiping down the counter.

But as she tidied, her thoughts slipped back into the deeper channels of her mind. Delia, Agatha, Ingrid – they were all grappling with the enormity of their legacy.

She shook her head, as if physically shaking off the cloud of anxiety that had begun to form. "One thing at a time, Marjie," she whispered to herself, but the whisper sounded loud in her ears, almost a plea. It was a strategy that had served her well over the years – focus on the here and now, and let tomorrow's battles fight themselves when the sun rose again.

Papa Jack rose, finishing his tea and setting down the cup. "I'd best be on my way. Thank you for the tea, Marjie," he said warmly, his eyes seeking hers for a brief moment, as if trying to read the scrolls of her worries.

"You're always welcome, my dear," she said, returning his gaze with a steadfastness that masked her inner turmoil.

He left, and as the door closed behind him, Marjie was left alone with her thoughts again, amidst the buzz of her bustling tea shop.

Yet, for all its vibrancy, its fragrances, its warmth, it couldn't quite fill the empty space his departure had created.

CHAPTER 3
DELIA

As soon as the paperwork was signed on the house rental, Delia walked the short distance into Myrtlewood Village. She still had over an hour to kill before her meeting with the lawyer Gillian had thoughtfully set up for her.

After the big breakfast, Delia wasn't yet hungry, so she decided to peruse the shops. It was a tiny village, but despite that, there was a reasonably good variety of shops.

First of all, she called into the apothecary. A beautiful young woman with long, wavy blonde hair gently explained a number of different remedies and products to her. She bought some fabulous skin cream and a tonic for peaceful sleep, hoping it might help with her nightmares.

Next door there was an ice cream shop which was closed, perhaps not so popular in the winter. Next, Delia dropped into the chocolate shop that belonged to Rosemary,

Marjie's good friend. It was currently staffed by a young man who looked a little like Papa Jack. He offered her hot chocolate, which she politely rain checked on, opting instead to buy herself some treats for later and also some for the children.

She tried to call Gillian while sitting on a bench overlooking the grassy lawn in the centre of the town, but there was no answer. Delia left a message telling her the good news about the house and how the children could come and stay anytime once she'd settled in.

Delia almost popped into the adorable looking bookshop, but seeing that Liam was there, she decided they'd seen rather enough of each other for the morning, and it might seem as if she was stalking him.

Without much else to do, Delia decided to visit Marjie's teashop for another coffee, or perhaps a tea, as she might well be over-caffeinated by now.

It was as she sank into a chair after dismissing Marjie's offers of several types of cakes and pastries that it hit her: Delia had somehow signed up for an entirely new life without really thinking it through.

Delia's career had been such a major focus in her life. Was she really now some retired lady with no job?

Magic was all well and good, but her whole life she'd been working hard, achieving great feats in the theatre. She was renowned for *her* company which Jerry was trying to take from her. She'd done brilliant things.

It was part of her identity, part of what she wanted to give to the world.

Theatre wasn't just entertainment. It was deeper. It was storytelling that made an impact on people. It was curating an experience that made people question, laugh, and gasp and think about things differently, see themselves and their lives in another way.

Theatre could be transformational, not just for the actors and the director, but for all the people who came to see it, experiencing the story much more poignantly than it would be on a flat screen.

Delia had thought about getting into movies, though. Movies could reach even greater audiences. She'd only been involved in a few short experimental films but she'd always wondered when Hollywood would come knocking, wanting her to take one of her plays to the big screen.

She'd had dreams, and they'd all vanished in a puff of magical smoke and a bad divorce. She sighed and took a sip of the tea that Marjie had brought her, along with a large slice of sponge drizzled with berry sauce and a big dollop of fresh cream which she had definitely not ordered. It looked delicious, though she wasn't sure she could fit it in after that big breakfast.

Delia scowled jokingly at Marjie, who laughed. "Just try it," Marjie insisted, and Delia decided that she could have a little taste after all.

It was delicious.

She'd inhaled the entire piece, light as air, before she'd even realised it.

As she nibbled the final crumbs, Delia pondered the destruction of her life as she knew it. She was torn. Of course, she didn't have to stay in Myrtlewood.

Sure, she'd rented a house, but it wasn't permanent.

Was staying here even for a few months giving up something that she could never reclaim? It wasn't too late to go back to London. Even if she had to start from scratch. She could rebuild her company. She could reclaim her career. The problem was she didn't know whether she *wanted* to.

The theatre was a harsh mistress. All those late nights, endless rehearsals, grinding herself to the bone, and all those arrogant actors – though many were lovely to work with, and she preferred to choose those ones for the good roles.

"I think you need some of my special remedy, dear," said Marjie, bringing her another pot of tea.

"Oh yes," said Delia. "You're going to slip something into my drink like Ingrid?"

Marjie laughed. "Only if you want me to. It's a bit of a pick-me-up."

Delia sighed. "I don't know."

"Well, how about a chat then?" said Marjie, pulling up a chair. The tea shop seemed to be rather bustling.

Delia shrugged. "Sure, and I'll take a double of your special remedy."

"What is it that's got you frowning and sighing so much? Life changes?"

"You've hit the nail on the head," Delia said. "You know, I used to be someone, and I feel like I don't know who I am anymore."

"I can assure you that's not true," said Marjie. "Being someone means you're always in the process of becoming someone else. Life's not static."

"Of course," agreed Delia, taking a sip of fresh tea, feeling a slight wave of giddiness. "This is good stuff!"

"My specialty," Marjie beamed.

"Basically, my whole life, after I gave up acting, I was working towards being a great director. I had accolades, fans, people who showed up at all my plays; I had great reviews in the Times. Things were all up and down, of course. Some shows bombed on their opening night. But for the most part, I had something; I built something; I was someone."

"What happened to all that?" Marjie asked.

"Well, the divorce, for one thing. Jerry's trying to take everything from me."

Marjie gave her hand a sympathetic squeeze. "You think you might want to go back to that life?"

"That's the problem," said Delia. "In some ways, I want to, and I feel like I should. I feel like it's wrong to walk away from it. I could have another good decade left in me, even longer...And yet, when I think about all the hours of repetitive rehearsals, I just feel exhausted."

"It sounds like a break is just what you need," said Marjie. "Besides, you know we need you here."

"I don't think you need me at all," said Delia. "If I were to leave, you'd find some other crone."

"It's not that simple," said Marjie.

"Well then, that just complicates things further, doesn't it?" said Delia. "I'm torn between my own career and some role that you seem to have me pinned down to."

"Not me personally," said Marjie. "Just fate."

"Screw fate!" said Delia. "Fate can go stuff itself."

Marjie giggled.

"If I do all of this," said Delia, "...if we unlock the power of the crones, we defeat whatever the evil thing is. Does that mean I can go back to having a life that I choose?"

"Yes, you can do whatever you like," said Marjie. "Though you might find it's not the same thing that you wanted to do before. That's the great thing about taking a break. You get some perspective."

Delia blew out a long slow breath. "I'm just scared that the longer I stay away, the further my career slips from my grasp. I'll become a has-been, an old woman nobody wants to work with anymore, that nobody values. There was a time when I was the young, up-and-coming 'it girl', and now I can't even face the thought of directing another play. I wouldn't even know where to start in rebuilding my company. I don't know if I have the energy for it, and yet I can't bear to lose it."

"Life throws all kinds of tensions at us, doesn't it?" said

Marjie. "You know, I've had quite a few businesses in my time. Almost all of them failed miserably."

Delia gave her an empathetic smile.

Marjie continued, "We don't always get what we want."

"We don't always know what we want," said Delia. "Or sometimes we want too many things, and they're all contradictory."

"You could look at it that way," said Marjie. "You know, you can write your own narrative. You can write the play of your own life, to use a more theatrical analogy. You get to tell the story in the way that makes sense for you. You could say that you're a washed-up old lady that nobody cares about."

"I didn't go that far!" said Delia.

"You know what I mean," Marjie continued. "You could say that you're being thrown around by the currents of fate. Your life is out of your control, that you never get anything that you want. You could complain, you could worry about possibilities slipping away from you and your career. You could give up and hide under the blankets. You could complain about all these grumpy old crones that you have to hang out with now because the fate of the world hangs in the balance—"

Delia chucked. "Is it really that dire?"

"Or," said Marjie, "you could say you're a *strong* woman, with a great past experience, with whole new opportunities on your horizon, and in the privileged position where you can take a holiday and relax. Think about what you really want to do. And then, when the time is right, and the stars align, you'll be in the right position to do it. Don't let anyone else tell the story for you. It's your story. You get to decide. This is your time. One of the great things about getting older is that you no longer have to be a good daughter, or fulfil the expectations that everyone had for you when you were younger. You get to decide your own expectations, on your own terms. You get to do whatever you like, if you can afford it."

"I don't know if I can," said Delia. "You know, it's silly. I just went and signed that lease with all the confidence in the world, without even thinking about it. Maybe I wanted to impress that handsome young man, Liam."

"He's a charmer," said Marjie.

"That's right," Delia sighed. "Jerry's trying to take all of the money. I still have a lease in London that I might not be able to afford either."

"Well, you should go and talk to Perseus Burk about that," said Marjie. "He's the best there is."

"You know," Delia said, looking at her watch, "it's almost time that I do."

CHAPTER 4
THE ROGUE

Declan paced his old camp within the shadowy embrace of the forest, the familiar scent of damp earth and decayed leaves permeating the air. His mind churned.

The Order of Crimson was in chaos, their voices still ringing in his ears from his last encounter with them. He hoped they would forget about him and his contract.

The contract weighed on him heavily, regret gnawing at him for not setting a cut-off date. It had been a deliberate omission at the time. He had craved long-term immersion in work, relief from the agonising boredom of immortality, but now the work was a worse kind of torture.

He crouched down, reaching towards the earth, his hands quickly became coated in the grime of the forest as he began digging.

He poured water into the hole, the sensation of the cool

liquid against his skin grounding him momentarily. He muttered an incantation and the water's surface swirled with patterns. The forest around him, with its soft rustling sounds and distant bird calls, seemed to fall away as he focused on the vision unfolding before him.

Delia Spark.

He watched her appear through the water, expecting to find her terrified or harried. But there she was, as casual as ever, strolling through the streets of Myrtlewood.

The Order had been furious when they lost track of the Crones. Even Declan's magic couldn't help them locate the township.

The Crones' magic was powerful. Whatever they had unleashed in the library had rendered them invisible to their enemies. Respect for their power mingled with his frustration.

Declan was not their enemy. Not yet. Though that could shift at any moment.

Long ago he'd chosen to have no personal alignment. Navigating convictions was impossible without emotional intuition to guide him. Instead, he'd chosen neutrality after many decades of swaying either side of the moral compass.

This magic though...it was intriguing.

Invisibility...

If he had scried this image of the Delia right in front of the Cleric, the man would have seen nothing but the reflections of the trees and sky – never mind that she was the fire witch that they'd sought for weeks.

In the chaos, Declan had taken temporary leave of his work and retreated to the one place the Order would not be able to find him.

They'd been trying to enter the township to no avail; it was simply as if Myrtlewood did not exist to them. For now.

Declan couldn't even speak of the Crones in front of the Order. He felt the thick magic of the Crones wrapping around his tongue, stifling his words even at the thought.

He watched Delia stroll along, into the quaint shops, purchasing scented candles, ointments, and truffles. Shopping? She was shopping! A fury ignited within him at the sight, reminding him of his earlier years of immortality, a time when his rage at mortals and their frivolous existence had grown to fever pitch.

His vision darkened at the memory.

He had become a ruthless force, a tempest of destruction. The horrendous and violent actions of his past were now confined to legend, but this new rage threatened to unleash his brutal nature again.

He hadn't yet decided whether that was something he wanted.

He continued to watch Delia, her carefree behaviour tearing at him. How could she be so nonchalant when everything she loved and cared about was at stake? The invisibility of the Crones might be protecting her and the township for now, but she was human, with connections beyond Myrtlewood, and the Order would find a way to break through the Crone's magic eventually. In all his years Declan had seldom seen a more well-resourced operation. At times they seemed bumbling, but even then, he had a creeping suspicion that all of it – down to the last misstep – was calculated and deliberate, as if someone higher up was pulling the strings, only letting the underlings know exactly what they needed to know to fail in the right way.

Declan shook his head. Surely he was imagining it. Yet, his instincts helped him sniff out strategy, and the Order had plenty of it.

It was only a small concern, compared to his rising rage.

He swiped at the surface of the water, bursting the illusion back to a simple reflection. Whatever was happening within him, it was connected to *her*.

Delia Spark was a menace, and whatever she was doing, it had to be stopped.

Over the centuries, all his emotions had blurred and then faded like etchings in worn leather until he could no longer sense them. The rage was the last to go, and yet, now, hundreds of years later it had surfaced again, tearing at him, burning him.

He couldn't fathom why this was happening, why he was so bound to this village even though he could be awaiting communications elsewhere. The Order didn't know he was here, so why did he keep returning to Myrtlewood? It made no sense. He only knew he could not leave. The cool breeze and the gentle sounds of the forest did nothing to distract him from the questions gnawing at him. He had his own mysteries to unravel.

CHAPTER 5
DELIA

Delia had a strangely giddy sensation running through her as she made her way to the lawyer's office. She wondered if Marjie had a habit of slipping things into people's drinks before they went to important meetings.

Perhaps it wasn't such a good idea to drink the special tea, but at least she was feeling better about her life.

Delia pushed her way through the heavy old wooden doors of the office and gave her name to the rather icy woman behind the counter who gestured for her to wait.

Delia took one of the two leather armchairs and pretended to read a magazine while secretly she was people watching the only person in view – the receptionist with her white-blonde bob and excellent posture, who seemed to be spending a lot of time filing her nails.

Maybe I can get a job like that, Delia pondered. *If I need money urgently to pay the rent...Maybe a job where I could just read all day... That would be marvellous.*

Delia glanced down at the magazine she was holding and almost dropped it before flicking through excitedly.

Instead of the outdated fashion brochure she expected, she found she'd inadvertently picked up *Magical You* – a legitimately mystical publication, by the looks of it.

On the front was an old woman with silver hair and startling blue eyes. It seemed to relate to the feature advertised. "Winter: The Season of The Crone" sat boldly amid the other articles – "How to Befriend Your Local Pixies", "Decoration Charms to Make Your Yule Really Pop", "Festive Recipes for a Wonderful Winter Feast", and "Five Fae Beauty Tips to Have You Looking Fabulous".

Delia's eyes bulged in surprise. She was tempted to slip the whole artefact into her handbag. She wanted to read every one of their ridiculous sounding articles, but flipped immediately to the feature on Crones and began reading:

The winter, of course, is associated with the time of Crones. The year has come to its completion through the new life of spring, the ripening of summer, the harvest of autumn, right through to the full matura-tion of life, before it is reborn again. We celebrate the solstice of winter, the time in which crone magic is strongest. Around the world, crone power has been awakening. This most ancient and protective of magics connects us, not only with our ancestors, but with the wise elders among us who are charged with guiding, protecting, and leading us to a better future.

Delia scoffed. WISE was the last thing she felt about now. Though she had to admit that it was nice that she seemed to have immersed herself accidentally in a subculture that valued older people and not just in a passing fad kind of way.

She read on about crone goddesses, the Cailleach, Cerridwen, and others. There was nothing in the article that gave her much of a clue as to her own magic, or the deeper power they were trying to unlock. But what could she expect from a magazine that seemed to be largely fashion and beauty tips with a few recipes?

Still, Delia did wonder if the lawyer's office would miss it. She nudged the copy gently towards her handbag, thinking she could always return it later after she'd read the whole thing. It was far too interesting to leave behind.

Just as she began to quietly commit minor theft, there was a sound of a throat clearing. Delia looked up and almost jumped, shocked to find a tall and handsome man standing only three metres away.

Delia glanced down at the half-stolen magazine and then back up into steely eyes.

"You're most welcome to take that," he said. "Cilla only leaves them here when she's finished with them."

The woman behind the desk, obviously Cilla, rolled her eyes and then returned her attention to her nails.

"Oh, right...Ugh, Okay. Thank you. I'm sorry," said Delia. "I was just so intrigued. I would have brought it back. Probably not the best start to a meeting with a lawyer."

The man quirked his mouth into a small smile. "Believe me, lawyers deal with a lot worse. Besides, I prefer when my clients are honest – at least with me – then I know more about the risks we're taking with any legal action ahead. There's nothing worse than someone slipping up and blurting out the truth in front of a judge without telling me first."

Delia stood up and shook the hand he offered.

"Perseus Burk," he said.

"Delia. Last name to be determined, but probably Spark," she replied. "And I'm making a note to be as honest with you as I can be."

"Excellent," he said, and led the way towards the grand corner office with a lovely view out towards the countryside behind the town.

"Gillian sent me the files," said Perseus Burk, gesturing to a thick manilla folder full of paper.

"It's rather a lot, isn't it?" said Delia. "Have you read all that?"

"Briefly," Mr Burk answered.

"And your conclusion? Am I doomed?"

He raised an eyebrow. "I like your candour. I must say, your ex-husband has made a meal of this. It's indeed made things look rather dire."

Delia felt herself deflate; all those years working towards something had been pulled out from underneath her. Her ex was taking it all. Everything seemed to have gone up in a great big bonfire, just like the one she had made of Jerry's and his mistress's clothing in the theatre that night.

"He's trying to argue that you've defamed him," Mr Burk continued. "And that the company is now worthless."

"Yes, I know that," said Delia, "but he's wrong."

"Naturally," he replied. "We're going to argue that all you did was draw some extra publicity. All publicity is good publicity, right?"

"Not exactly," said Delia with a sigh. "But it's better than obscurity."

The lawyer continued, "Nothing you did threatened the reputation of the company itself because it wasn't directly related to any performance. Other than your husband being a bad actor. I believe we can argue that he was the one who sabotaged the company. And that you should get everything."

"Everything?" Delia asked, shocked.

Mr Burk pressed his hands together and furrowed his brow. "Well, I suppose he'd get to keep half the value of the house and your collective investments and savings."

"But you think I could get my fair share...and the company?" Delia asked.

In that moment, that was all she cared about. Yet, with a second thought, it was daunting. That meant going back to London, leaving this strange and magical place behind. How frustrating it was to want everything and yet nothing at the same time. To be so excited and yet overwhelmed and exhausted. To simultaneously yearn to throw in the towel and burn down one's entire old life, while also longing to keep all of it.

To have it all.

To experience every moment.

To lose nothing.

Something's got to give, she told herself.

"Your husband's made a series of poor decisions," said Mr Burk.

"I see...I mean of course he has," said Delia. "But what are you talking about in particular?"

The lawyer smiled slightly. "We're going to argue that he made terrible business decisions, that he's the one who put the company at risk. I have an entire folder of examples that Gillian compiled."

Delia felt her heart warm. Gilly had been doing all this – working away behind the scenes, to support her mother despite being strangely distant in all of the chaos in her life, moving towns with her two small children.

When her daughter had first become distant, Delia had suspected she'd taken Jerry's side in the divorce, but then again,

Gillian and her father had never been close. He'd always wanted a boy in a stereotypical sexist way that made Delia feel slightly ill. Jerry had kept his distance from her and from Delia too, really. He'd immersed himself in work at any possible opportunity – work or affairs which he seemed to treat with the same grim determination as any other job or food and exercise regime. Delia often wondered what she'd seen in him in the first place.

But Gilly helping Delia now showed that she cared. She couldn't work the case because it was a conflict of interest, but she'd done all this background digging. She'd been through all the company records that Delia's assistant had meticulously kept, including the ones that Jerry tried to keep secret. However, one can't keep credit cards secret. There was always a paper trail.

"What's this?" Delia asked, picking up a black folder.

"That was from the private investigator you daughter hired to tail him," Mr Burk replied. "She was wondering what he was doing with his cash withdrawals."

Delia felt her heart melt with tenderness. "She really does care," she blurted out loud before covering her mouth.

Mr Burk gave her a long, serious look. "Of course she does. She loves you very much. She's going through some...changes, as I understand it."

"Of course," said Delia. "You know her well, then?"

Of course Gilly was going through changes with her own marriage ending, a new job, and moving house, but what did this man know of it, and how well did he really know Gillian?

"No, not really," said Mr Burk. "Only in a collegial capacity."

Delia looked at the handsome lawyer. "You don't happen to be single, do you?"

His expression made her laugh. "No, not for me," said Delia. "Gosh, think of the age difference!"

He shot her an awkward look.

Delia giggled. "I was just thinking Gillian might need a new romantic interest to keep her occupied. Take her mind off that oaf she married."

Mr Burk's expression was inscrutable. And then he coughed again. "I can assure you that I'm not single."

"That's a shame," said Delia, still giddy from the tea. "You don't happen to have any brothers, do you?"

"Not anymore," said Mr Burk.

"Oh, I'm sorry. This is all terribly inappropriate," said Delia. "At least I didn't set you on fire, yet."

Mr Burk gave her a piercing look. "Is that something you do?"

Delia sighed. "You work in this town. You must be something magical, right?"

The lawyer shrugged nonchalantly.

"Okay, full disclosure," said Delia. "You might as well know. I'm some kind of crone-witch thing. I didn't know about it until very recently. Gilly doesn't know anything – don't tell her."

"Of course not," said Mr Burk. "I wouldn't dream of it. Client confidentiality is of the utmost importance."

"Just in the last few weeks," Delia explained, "I started accidentally setting things on fire when I'm angry."

"I'll be sure not to anger you, then," he replied, "and wear flame retardant clothing."

Delia took a sharp breath. "That would be wise. So, you think we've got a case? And it's not just a hopeless stab in the dark? I need a really bloodthirsty lawyer."

Mr Burk coughed, almost as if he was choking.

"I don't mean that as an insult," she quickly added. "It's a good thing."

He nodded slowly. "I'm not going to give you any false hope. Your husband has very expensive and powerful legal representation. But I think he's made enough poor decisions with the business that I think you have a shot. Besides, if he's arguing it's no longer worth anything, he should have no trouble in letting it go."

Delia smiled. "I like you. But – not like that!"

"Understood," said Mr Burk, smiling subtly. "You'll be staying in Myrtlewood for the foreseeable future then?"

"I haven't quite decided," said Delia. "If what you say is true, and I could get my company back, well, I suppose I'll have to go back to London at some point, but I'm on a bit of a sabbatical, you might say."

He nodded.

"Err...If you see Gillian, tell her I'm settling in nicely."

"I'll do that," he said warmly, for someone typically so cool – even his handshake had been freezing. She wondered whether he'd seen a doctor about his circulation. However, that, just like his relationship status, was none of her business, so she decided not to pry further. "So...what's the next step?"

Mr Burk looked her in the eye. "I say we file some rather damning paperwork and then give them a couple of weeks to stew over it before we convince them to settle on our terms."

"Won't that give them more time to prepare?" Delia asked.

Mr Burk pressed his hands towards his chin. "Yes, but we can predict what that will be and start preparing in advance. Just let me know if you have any skeletons in your closet."

Delia winced, wondering about all the slightly dubious things she'd done over the years. Stealing a magazine from a lawyer's office was one thing...getting drunk with Kitty led to all kinds of shenanigans. Whatever trouble she'd got herself into in the past might surface and rear its ugly head in front of a judge. "I don't want to think about it," she muttered.

"Take your time. I'm a very patient lawyer, you'll find," he assured her.

"That's a good quality to have, one that I'm not so blessed with," Delia admitted. "But all right. We'll do things your way. You seem like you know what you're doing."

"I do have rather a lot of experience, I assure you," Burk confirmed.

Delia smiled at him. "Excellent. Well, if there's nothing else..."

"Not today," Mr Burk said and showed her out of his office.

Delia opened the doors and blinked in the bright sunlight. It had been a little bit dark in there. She wondered whether they could renovate, bring a bit more light into the place. They seemed to have enough money judging by the decor.

She looked around at the little village that was her temporary home and decided that regardless of the future, she was going to enjoy herself and her sabbatical as much as possible.

CHAPTER 6
AGATHA

Agatha Twigg's kitchen was a welcoming blend of cosy charm and disorganised clutter, a reflection of a woman who spent more time in her library than fussing over her farmhouse's decor.

The table was laden with a late breakfast of toast, marmalades, and steaming tea. Her niece, Marla, a tiny woman with a penchant for cardigans and a reptilian air about her, was holding forth about the current state of affairs at Myrtlewood Academy. Agatha's ears were half-attuned to the complaints, but her thoughts were elsewhere, tangled in the budding pulse of crone magic. She could sense it growing within her.

"I tell you, Aunty, if we lose Athena Thorn and Elise Fern, we risk becoming second-rate among the global magical community!" Marla grumbled, her voice taking on a tone of exasperation. "They've both missed so much school in the last term..."

Agatha forced herself to focus, nodding thoughtfully at Marla's concerns. The toast on her plate seemed less appealing as she thought about the magic within her, how it connected to her new friends, Delia and Ingrid, and even Marjie, who she'd never considered more than an acquaintance before now.

A secret smile tugged at her lips at the thought of wrestling the grimoire from Ingrid's hands. She wanted that magic, needed to explore it more.

"I'm sure it will be all fine, Marla," Agatha reassured her niece, her voice soothing and calm. "They're just rather... occupied."

Agatha knew a lot more than her niece did, having been pulled into help with a rather unorthodox investigation involving both girls. She hadn't shared all the details with her niece as she held the private opinion that some things were more important than school attendance – such as one's personal study in solitude, or dangerous quests into the underworld.

Marla's eyes narrowed, her suspicion evident, but she sighed and relented. "You're rather jolly this morning."

"Am I?" said Agatha, wondering if it was the crone power messing with her. Perhaps she ought to put on a sterner demeanour just to be safe.

"What have you been occupied with over past few days?" Marla asked, and not for the first time.

"Just visiting with friends," Agatha said curtly.

"It's not like you to have friends, plural," Marla quipped.

"That's none of your concern. And as for the school girls,

they will be fine, so don't concern yourself with them either. Worrying tends to be a pointless waste of time, not befitting a Twigg."

Marla sighed. "I suppose you're right, Aunty. But they're such promising students, and losing them would be a blow to the Academy."

Agatha reached across the table, patting Marla's hand in a rare gesture of affection. "Don't fret, my dear. Things have a way of working out, especially in Myrtlewood..."

Agatha's voice trailed off, and her thoughts drifted back to the grimoire, the ancient power they'd awakened. She felt it like a song in her veins, a call to something greater.

The world of magic was vast and mysterious, and she was on the brink of something extraordinary. Her breakfast with Marla seemed trivial in comparison, but family was family, and she kept her thoughts and feelings to herself, content to listen to Marla's concerns and offer comfort where she could. The secrets of the crones would remain locked away for now.

CHAPTER 7
DELIA

Delia yawned and looked out through the windows. She'd forgotten to draw the curtains the night before, and was delighted to see snow floating dreamily through the air, the trees and roofs nearby frosted in white like the icing on a cartoon cake.

It hadn't taken long to settle into her new house. In fact, by the first evening, she'd practically moved in, as all that entailed was ferrying her suitcase from the pub.

However, she was rather low on clothing.

Having only planned a short trip, she hadn't packed enough, and she was uncertain whether it would be safe to return to her London apartment for more.

She didn't want to risk sending her best friend, Kitty, or anyone else into potential danger. Unfortunately, there wasn't much in the way of clothes-shopping in Myrtlewood unless you were after a felt cape or other ceremonial garments.

Marjie had offered to lend her anything she needed, but Delia shuddered at the thought of more bright floral dresses, even bewitched to be grey. Marjie was a sweet creature, but Delia had rather different taste.

So, until she could visit the nearest city and find more clothing, Delia was stuck wearing the same three outfits, which, for now, suited her just fine.

Despite nearly everyone in Myrtlewood's obsession with tea, Delia found a stove-top espresso maker among the kitchen items that came with the house. Clearly, Liam's mother was more cosmopolitan than her fellow Myrtlewood citizens.

Delia resolved to pick up ground coffee beans from the local grocery store, which was only a casual walk away, and brew herself a robust beverage. She enjoyed the walk. The gentle winter breeze refreshed her as pale sunlight filtered through the scattering snowflakes, grateful she'd brought at least one good winter coat and gloves with her.

Snow had fallen in the night but the roads and footpaths were cleared, as if by magic – well, probably, it was by magic.

Back in the comfort of the house, Delia smiled as she made herself a nice coffee with cream.

She sat in the sunroom overlooking the back garden.

Yes, it was frosty and icy outside, but the sunroom was delightfully warm with glowing golden light amplified through the glass.

The house didn't seem to get properly cold, and Delia wondered whether it was some kind of magical charm that kept it a comfortable temperature, as she could find no signs of heating control other than the fireplace.

She sighed happily as she sipped her coffee.

Life hadn't felt this good for quite a long time, despite the highs and lows of the theatre. Delia couldn't remember the last time she'd felt so content.

There was nothing she had to do, nowhere she had to be.

Just then, her phone rang, blaring out the *Star Wars* music that Delia didn't have the heart to change because it reminded her of her rather aloof daughter and grandchildren. She wondered how little Merryn and Keyne were coping with all the change, then quickly pulled her mind back before she got too caught up in missing them.

"Delia!" Kitty growled into the phone.

"I'm sorry...I'm so sorry," Delia said. "I should have returned your calls."

"Ridiculous! I've been to your apartment five times!"

"I told you I was away."

"I expected you to be back by now!"

Delia heart started to race as Kitty's earlier words sunk in. "I think you should stay away from my apartment."

"Why?" Kitty asked in a demanding tone.

"It's a shady building." Delia's tone sounded weak, even to her.

"Really?" Kitty said. "What makes you say that? You're being paranoid again. You told me Jerry sent some thespians after you."

"Well..." Delia struggled to find a plausible explanation. How could she tell her oldest friend that those 'thespians' had actually been the foot soldiers of an ancient magical secret society? Kitty had been incredulous enough when she thought it was just actors. "Err, I think it's more complicated than that."

Kitty made an unimpressed groan. "Darling, we really must get your mental health checked. I'm worried about you."

"Don't start," Delia retorted. "I'm perfectly fine. I'm just on holiday, and I will be for a long time."

She could tell Kitty was glaring as silence ensued. Delia allowed the silence to elapse. There was nothing she could say to take Kitty's worries away. *A caring best friend is a force to be reckoned with.*

"I'm a little hurt you didn't invite me to come with you," Kitty admitted. "Maybe I could pop down and visit if you're planning on sticking around in the country for a while." Her voice was thick with distain, as though Delia had abandoned her life in London to become a farm hand, as if she might arrive to find her knee-deep in mud in a pigsty.

"I don't think it's your style," Delia said, playing on Kitty's disapproval for anything that wasn't posh city life. "Just be careful, okay? I really do think there are some dodgy people around. You haven't been followed or anything, have you? I know it *sounds* paranoid but..."

Kitty sighed with sarcasm. "I'm perfectly fine and capable of looking after myself. You, on the other hand, are a liability."

Delia sighed. "Look, it's been a difficult time. I'm just finding my feet."

"Good," said Kitty. "And when you've found them, be sure to walk them right back *here*." There was a moment of silence and then she added, "I miss you."

"I miss you too," Delia admitted.

For a moment, she wanted nothing more than to tell Kitty everything, including about her new friends. However, not only was the story *far* too strange to adapt to a mundane version, but she also didn't want her best and oldest friend to think she'd abandoned her for a new social group.

She reached for careful words to placate Kitty. "Once I'm settled in...maybe you could come to visit."

"That makes it sound like you're going to be staying for a while."

"I think I am," Delia admitted, trying to ignore the obvious pout in her friend's voice. "I really need some time to straighten myself out. Get grounded, you know?"

Another moment of heavy silence followed.

"Alright, then," said Kitty. "Just promise me you're not going to let Jerry rip you off. He's an awful prick. He deserves a cutthroat lawyer going for the jugular."

Delia smiled. "You know, I just met with a lawyer who I think will do the trick, besides..." Her heart warmed. "You know, Gillian's done all this wonderful background research for me. I thought we were growing apart and that she didn't care. But it turns out she just needs her space too. And she's done lots to help. She even hired a private investigator."

"Oh, how sweet," Kitty replied, without the sarcasm this time. "I told you it would work out. Gillian's got a good head on her shoulders."

Delia wanted to say more. Far too much more. However, she decided to hang up the phone after making promises to stay in better touch and asking Kitty to do her a big favour, which would at least keep her feeling useful, occupied, and relevant.

"It would be amazing if you could sort out getting someone in to clean out my old apartment. I need to end the lease."

"You're not moving to the countryside permanently?" Kitty sounded outraged.

"No. It's just...It's a terrible building."

"That's true," Kitty conceded. "We'll find you something much nicer once the settlement comes through. Sure, I'll sort out your baggage for you while you swan around on holiday."

"Thanks," said Delia. "But don't go there yourself. I'm serious. There are risks. Hire some movers, you know? Get the key from the leasing agent. I'll send them an email."

"I still don't like how this all sounds so serious and permanent," Kitty noted, her voice imbued with a sense of urgency more suited to a serious accident than a new life in the countryside.

"I'm not really in a position to make long-term decisions

right now," Delia admitted. "I just need to get a bit of closure first. It has been a rather turbulent time."

"Of course, it has," Kitty agreed. "It's been hell. You do what you need to do. I'll sort it out for you."

Delia hung up the phone, feeling so much lighter.

She didn't like the fact that Kitty had visited her apartment. What if the Order of Crimson had been watching? But perhaps if they'd only seen her knocking on the door, they'd assume she wasn't important enough for Delia to keep her in the know. She felt a pang of guilt for treating her best and oldest friend so poorly, but she hoped that made it seem like Kitty was no more than a persistent fan or acquaintance.

She took a deep breath and finished her coffee, pushing her guilt and worries out of her mind. This was no time for dwelling on things she couldn't control.

She gazed back out the window at the lovely view of the snow-covered park, appreciating that she had an opportunity to feel blissful contentment. If she could only just relax and return to that state, she could actually enjoy herself.

However, her aspirations towards a peaceful life were promptly disrupted by a knock on the door.

CHAPTER 8
THE SHEPHERD

The Order of Crimson's compound loomed, an austere fortress bearing the weight of centuries, set atop a secluded plateau. Its high stone walls, adorned with ancient runes and wards, shielded mystical gardens and training grounds, the structures within, forged through discipline and tradition. Beyond the open courtyards, a labyrinth of shadowed hallways and hidden chambers beckoned, secrets whispered in the corners, where cobwebs met aged wood.

Father Benedict scowled at the chaos that had crept into the Order. He looked around the room he'd sequestered. Tall shelves groaned under the weight of arcane tomes, scrolls, and mysterious artefacts, while a heavy oak table stood in the centre, its surface etched with maps and diagrams. The scents of old parchment, burning candles, and alchemical brews lingered in the air, mingling with the soft glow that emanated from the narrow, leaded windows. Time itself seemed to pause here, in a room where the echoes of past triumphs and failures still resonated, lingering like a haunting melody.

He had done his best to whip the room into shape.

In a world where chaos often reigned supreme, the compound of the Order of Crimson should shine like a beacon of *order.*

Indeed, Father Benedict's strategy room was a marvel of meticulous planning. It was a testament to control and precision. Scrolls were lined up with the kind of accuracy that would make a mathematician weep with joy, maps were stretched taut and pinned at the corners with a uniformity that defied normal physics, and even the quills in their ink pots stood at attention, bristles combed and aligned. All drafts had been stopped so that the candle flames wouldn't flicker. They stood in place, burning with a sort of regulated attention. Everything was positioned, prepared, and polished to an exacting standard. It was an environment where chaos was not merely kept at bay; it was given a stern look, and sent to stand in the corner to think about what it had done.

Father Benedict stood rigid at the head of the table, his hands clenched behind his back, eyes ablaze with frustration.

This newly arranged chamber for Operation Theta was empty apart from an air of anticipation. The table was full of inked parchment, tangible records of the Order's meticulous planning, but his mind was seething in chaos.

The elusive fire witch and her new Crone friends had defied

all his calculations and predictions. He had studied her exten-
sively, trying to predict her movements, believing he understood
her nature. But fire was unpredictable, and Delia had proven to
be more so.

Despite all his years of meticulous research on her, sacri-
ficing himself for the greater good of the Order and the future of
the world, Father Benedict could no more determine her next
move than he could plot the movements of a wildfire. All his
precision and attention to detail was wasted on this absolutely
chaotic monster.

He took a deep breath and raised his hand to his forehead in
despair.

The door creaked open, breaking his train of thought.

The Cleric entered, his appearance slightly bumbling, his
eyes filled with uncertainty.

"Shepherd," the Cleric stammered, barely lowering his head
in a bow, his voice wavering.

"A report?" Father Benedict asked curtly.

"There has been no change in the situation."

The Shepherd's scowl deepened. "That is nothing to
report."

"It's as if the crones simply vanished, along with the entire
town of Myrtlewood and the area around it."

Father Benedict's jaw tightened, his eyes never leaving the
table, his mind racing.

The Cleric continued, "Every attempt we've made to enter
the township over the past few days has strangely led our

soldiers back the way they came, or they found themselves further up the coast."

"This is not useful information," Father Benedict declared.

"Do you think the town has moved?" the Cleric asked, a hint of desperation in his voice. "Could it have been transported elsewhere?"

"No," Father Benedict replied, his voice calm and measured, masking the storm of emotions within him. "The ancient magic is powerful – but it is cloaking magic, and there will be a way to break it, even if it requires somewhat unorthodox methods."

The Cleric's eyes lit up in anticipation, but Father Benedict wasn't about to let him in on any of his secrets. Instead, he cast his eyes over the table, his mind sharpening, the tactical approach forming. The scrolls and maps seemed to beckon him, the answers lying within their intricate details. There was one missing piece: the fire witch.

Delia Spark.

The was the weak point in the Crones. So new to the world of magic and with powers she could not control. He needed to find a way to lure her out.

His previous failures and recent setbacks were mere lessons, learning experiences that would ultimately lead to triumph. He had the wisdom, the strategy, the purpose. He was the Crimson Shepherd, and he would lead the Order to victory.

Despite his silence, the air seemed to hum with energy, the air thick with the weight of impending action. Father Benedict felt a surge of determination, a renewed sense of purpose.

Operation Theta was in motion, and he would not be deterred.

He turned to the Cleric, his eyes gleaming with resolve. "Prepare the next phase. We must be relentless. We must be precise. We will find a way to break the cloaking, and we will find Delia."

The Cleric nodded, bolstered by the Shepherd's unwavering conviction. The room, filled with the tangible presence of their combined will, seemed to echo with a silent promise.

The Order of Crimson would prevail. They would bring the Crones to justice and right the balance of the world. The game was far from over, and Father Benedict was ready to make his next move.

CHAPTER 9
DELIA

Delia was almost at the door. "I'm coming," she called out.

Marjie bustled in with Agatha trailing close behind.

"This place isn't too bad," Marjie remarked, glancing around. "It's not quite as homey as mine."

"That's for certain," said Agatha wryly.

"Not that I have a house anymore." Marjie's voice dropped to a murmur.

"I'm sorry about that," Delia said, but Marjie shook her head, dismissing the apology.

"No, it was for the best. Sometimes it's better to burn your past right down to the ground."

"You know, I'm starting to feel that way," Delia confessed.

Agatha nodded, understanding the sentiment. "I'm glad to

hear it," she said, before glancing around the room. "Have you got any tea?"

Marjie tutted. "Don't be rude!"

Before Delia could respond, Marjie announced, "I did bring some tea, if you need any."

"I suppose we're having tea then." Delia led them back to the sunroom, which was no longer as peaceful as it had been moments before. "To what do I owe the honour of this visit?" she asked.

Marjie smiled. "Nothing pressing, dear. We just wanted to call in and see how you were doing."

"And?" Delia asked.

"We need to prepare," Agatha added, bringing the conversation back to serious matters. "The winter solstice is coming up this weekend."

"Of course," Delia replied. "That's when the Crone powers are strongest." She almost sounded as if she knew what she was talking about, aided by the waiting-room magazine's article.

Agatha gave a curt nod. "Besides, Ingrid invited us to tea tomorrow, remember?"

"Oh yes." Delia smiled, noticing how pleased Marjie looked. "We don't really know what we're dealing with. So preparing seems a bit tricky,"

"That's what I tried to tell her," said Agatha. "But Marjie's on edge because of the underworld and those Thorn women."

"I don't want to talk about it," said Marjie anxiously. "I just need a distraction."

"Perhaps if we write down everything that we do know, we can figure out what we don't know," Delia suggested.

"That sounds sensible," said Agatha.

"Uhh, Delia. There's something else I should tell you about," said Marjie. "I thought it might scare you off so I didn't say anything before, but I suppose you probably ought to know."

"What is it?" Delia asked.

"Oh, you mean about the trouble around Myrtlewood that we've been helping Rosemary with?" said Agatha. "Oh yes, nasty business."

"More trouble," said Delia, raising both eyebrows.

Marjie shook her head. "It's probably nothing. I mean, nothing to do with us at least. But there have been some err... terrible things happening in Myrtlewood, suspiciously related to winter, and magically caused."

Delia narrowed her eyes. "Why are you telling me this now?"

Marjie shot her a reassuring smile. "Forget I said anything, dear. Those problems are probably nothing to do with the Order at all. Their magic is definitely different."

"And the winter solstice?" Delia asked.

"Yes..." Marjie said slowly. "Well, there may be some connection; however, putting that aside for a moment—"

"Wait a minute," said Delia. "I think maybe I should know a little bit more..."

"No," Agatha said sternly. "We need to *focus*."

"Why not write down everything we know," Delia suggested.

"About the magic of the crones, you mean?" said Marjie.

"Don't be ridiculous," said Agatha. "What if somebody were to find the piece of paper?"

"They would think we were plotting a fantasy movie," said Marjie.

"It could be dangerous," Agatha warned. "If we don't write it down, then we'll just have to say it over and over to ourselves. So that we don't forget and make a mental list. Maybe a rhyme. That's how people remembered things in the old days before the invention of paper or even written language."

Marjie was smiling, but Delia could almost hear the eye roll.

"What about the dragons?" said Delia. "I want to know about them."

"The less we know, the better," Agatha grunted. "We want to stay as far away from dragons as possible. They're wicked beasts, dangerous and ghastly."

Delia shrugged and sipped the tea Marjie had mysteriously poured somehow while they were distracted with the conversation. And with that, Delia's peaceful morning turned into one of scheming, speculation, and planning.

CHAPTER 10
THE CLERIC

The Cleric sat before a rather unusual instrument, foreign to the dimly lit chambers of the Order, and utterly defiant of the traditional ways of magical communication.

It was a telephone, a device that looked innocent enough, but its purpose was perplexing and rather confounding to someone who'd always been taught to distrust the gimmicks of modern mundane technology.

A deep breath steadied his mind as he reached out to touch the contraption, feeling its plastic coolness under his fingertips. It was an alien sensation, something that didn't resonate with the natural flow of the magical world.

"Why would we ever use such a thing?" he muttered to himself, but the answer lay in the instructions given to him by the Shepherd.

The Shepherd's orders had been clear, although the Cleric couldn't help but feel a sense of confusion at their true purpose.

The plan involved booking a very specific theatre for the night of the Winter Solstice. He had no understanding of why, but the Shepherd had ominously said that he wanted to "hit the fire witch where it hurts".

The theatre, the Solstice, the fire witch – it all seemed to be a convoluted riddle.

The Cleric was not privy to the inner workings of Father Benedict's mind, and he didn't pretend to be. But obedience was his duty, and so he picked up the receiver and started dialling the number provided.

The sounds the telephone made were an odd music, and he waited impatiently for someone to answer on the other end.

"Good evening, how may I assist you?" a polite voice inquired. A woman.

The Cleric frowned. "I wish to book your establishment for the night of the Winter Solstice." His voice was imbued with a formality that was unintentionally intimidating.

There was a pause, followed by, "The winter..."

"The solstice of course. The twenty-first of December."

"That's rather soon, Sir. May I inquire as to the nature of your event?"

"It's a private affair," the Cleric stated firmly, unwilling to reveal more.

Moments passed in which the woman made clickety-clack noises, clearly using some other form of modern gadgetry.

The Cleric's face twisted in patient scorn.

"I'm afraid the theatre is booked until Christmas," she finally replied.

"Ah..." The Cleric had been warned by Father Benedict that this could be the case.

"Sir?"

"Ah, yes?" He fumbled with the small pouch the Crimson Shepherd had handed him, stalling for time. He had to keep her on the line. This was part of Father Benedict's instructions.

"Is there anything else I can help you with?" she asked, sounding tired, bored, or impatient, but trained to be polite.

"Yes..."

He drew the powder from the bag. It shimmered in his palm as he whispered the incantation in Latin.

"I didn't quite catch that, Sir..."

The powder floated in the air around the telephone and then flew into the receiver.

At the other end, the woman coughed.

"Apologies, Sir."

"We have an opening," the Cleric said firmly.

"We do?" the woman's voice sounded vague and confused.

"For winter solstice, yes."

"Of course, the solstice...What time was that again?"

"All day and into the evening," said the Cleric patiently, allowing a small smile to creep over his face. The Shepherd would surely be impressed.

The conversation continued, filled with questions that

seemed irrelevant to the Cleric. Yet he answered them, one by one, until the booking was complete. The Cleric hung up the receiver, a strange sense of accomplishment mixing with his lingering confusion.

He sat back in his chair, pondering the Shepherd's mysterious orders. The winter solstice was important, but why the theatre? And what did it have to do with the fire witch?

He glanced around his office, seeking comfort in the familiar surroundings filled with books, scrolls, and the gentle warmth of the fireplace. These were the things he understood, not the baffling world of telephones and theatres.

Yet he knew that the mission was evolving, and he had to adapt to the challenges it presented, even if they were wrapped in perplexity and intrigue.

CHAPTER II
DELIA

S now had fallen thicker overnight. Delia woke chilled and alert.

"Today, I'm finally going to do it," she vowed to herself.

She threw on the thick magenta dressing gown that Marjie had lent her. She made a hot thermos of coffee and trudged out to the back steps of the house carrying a little metal plate and a stack of paper.

She scrunched up the first ball of paper, carefully put it in the centre of the metal plate, and placed it on the ground.

She then stood back several metres. She'd been practicing every day, but it hadn't been without its minor disasters. In fact, the reason she felt the need to start so early in the morning after snowfall was because it seemed like the least flammable time imaginable.

Delia took a deep breath, pushing away the feelings of pressure she felt.

She was still yet to master her power, or any semblance of it, and today they were supposed to be having tea with Ingrid.

Delia hated feeling incompetent more than almost anything else. She didn't want her new friends to look down on her when they were all accomplished witches and she could barely set anything alight unless it was by accident. The only time she'd ever properly used her power deliberately was on the Cowboy, and that had been in the heat of battle. She needed more control. She needed mastery.

"Now listen here," she said to the piece of paper. "You know you want to burst into flames in a reasonable way. So, I'm just going to imagine..." She tried visualising the paper igniting.

This was a technique that had never worked for her in the past, but it seemed like it really ought to. She was a visual person after all. However, the piece of paper just sat there, scrunched, as if glaring back at her, unimpressed.

Marjie had offered her lots of advice, and Agatha had even given her a book on learning magic in later life. However, nothing Delia tried seemed to work.

When the visualisations failed yet again, she tried clicking her fingers, stomping her feet, commanding, demanding, pleading, begging, and finally, in a puff of rage, swearing loudly. At which point, a nearby rosebush that had been covered in snow burst into flames instead.

"Oh blast!" Delia said, grabbing one of the buckets of water she'd stacked up nearby. She threw it towards the rosebush, only to find that the top layer of water on the bucket had frozen solid.

Delia smacked the ice with her hands and then stomped on it to crack through, and tried again to tip it onto the burning bush. By the time she'd finally put the fire out, the bucket was starting to smoke of its own accord, and she herself was dishevelled, slightly damp, and singed.

"Delia?" a musical voice called out. Marjie poked her head out the back door. "Oh, there you are. Nobody answered when I knocked and I was worried you might have taken a fall."

"I didn't hear you, not that I'd want you to see me like this," Delia grumbled.

"Like what? You look perfectly fine," said Marjie.

"Don't lie."

"You've been practicing, haven't you?" said Marjie.

"Yes. And I'm a total failure. You might as well give up on me and find yourself another Crone."

"Nonsense," said Marjie. "Tell me what happened."

Delia sighed and recounted the story to Marjie between sips of strong coffee.

"I suppose I should offer you some tea," she muttered.

"Don't worry. I brought my own," said Marjie. "I *know* you're not really a tea drinker, but I don't hold it against you or anything."

"That's reassuring," said Delia flatly.

Marjie pulled an ornamental box out of her handbag which, like something out of Mary Poppins, quickly turned itself into a small table setting complete with a piping hot teapot, all in a pretty purple and gold pattern.

Delia narrowed her eyes. "So, you can do that and I can't even set a piece of paper on fire deliberately?"

"Oh, this isn't me," said Marjie. "No, my magic is really all about food, which is unfortunate, really."

"I don't know, I'm quite a fan," said Delia, nibbling at a scone from the plate that Marjie had set on the table.

Marjie smiled at her. "That's sweet of you to say. However, as much as I feel that it's true in my soul that I'm the water Crone – empathy, emotion, nurturing – despite all that, I don't really get along with *water* all that well. I'm not a big fan of the ocean. And as much as I've coached Rosemary to connect with the water, I can't say I have any great power over the element itself. At least *you* can set things on fire."

"Only when I get really angry," said Delia.

"And I suppose that's the secret," said Marjie. "You've got to connect with that anger. Master it. That way, you'll master your own magic."

"I don't particularly like my anger," Delia admitted. "I mean, having a fiery personality is one thing, but rage is hard to control."

"Just like fire," Marjie pointed out.

"You're right," said Delia. "It's far too hard, apparently. I've been practicing every day."

"That's good," said Marjie encouragingly.

"It's not good if I have nothing to show for it," Delia grumbled.

"Mastery takes time," said Marjie. "I'm sure if we carry on practicing and learning and trying new things, we'll both master our elements in no time."

Delia frowned. "You don't have to make me feel better by telling me that you don't know what you're doing either."

"I wish it was that simple," said Marjie. "Now, my magic has always been rather more subtle."

Delia sighed. "Based on your logic, I need to connect with my anger and rage in order to set things on fire deliberately."

"And your passion," Marjie added.

"Sure, all that," said Delia. "Well, if that's the case, maybe in order for you to connect with water more deeply, you need to connect with your heart. What does your heart want?"

Marjie had a slightly guilty expression on her face. "That's enough about me," she said. "Why don't you go on upstairs and get ready? Agatha will be here soon, and then we'll head off to see Ingrid."

Delia had the distinct impression that Marjie was trying to brush her off. She didn't really want to talk about whatever her heart desired. Fair enough. It was really none of Delia's business.

CHAPTER 12
INGRID

Ingrid scowled as she turned a page, carefully. She was ensconced within her woodland hut, walls lined with shelves replete with dusty tomes, jars of assorted herbs, and curious artefacts from all corners of the world. The smell of burning cedarwood wafted through the air from a small hearth in the corner, mingling with the aroma of herbs and dried flowers that hung from the ceiling. Her gaze remained fixed on the ancient grimoire of the Myrtlewood Crones. She'd been poring over it in her spare moments every day, looking for clues, endeavouring to fathom the arcane sigils and decipher the minute cursive scrawl.

Ingrid paused for a moment, taking in the atmosphere of her hut as if seeing it anew. The walls were made of weathered logs, layered with years of enchanted protection spells that had kept the house and its occupant safe from intruders and the elements alike. Small shelves jutted out of the walls, adorned with tiny clay pots filled with dried herbs – rosemary for protection, lavender for tranquillity, mugwort for visions, and more.

In the hearth, a softly crackling fire danced, imbued with a gentle spell to keep the room consistently warm without the need for constant tending. It emitted a slightly spicy, comforting smell, thanks to a bundle of sage and pine needles Ingrid had thrown in earlier. The familiar scent melded with the richer, darker aroma of ancient parchment and ink that seemed to almost ooze from the ancient grimoire on her wooden desk.

Adjusting her monocle, she leaned in to read several passages, intoning in an antiquated form of English:

Whan Wynter Solstice graces sky,
Forsooth, second stage of Crone might nigh.
Foure houses of witcherye birth,
Harbour seeds of Crone's true worth.

The passage she just read seemed to suggest that the Crones' power was divided, perhaps hidden within the cyclical seasons, each providing a different key to their full potential. She pondered on this, her eyes roaming back to the aged parchment.

The winter solstice being pivotal for the next stage of unlocking Crone power was no revelation to her; it was, after all, something she'd assumed. Winter was the time of crones. But the book had more to unfold – this matter of the Myrtlewood

Crone powers being embedded within four witching families was a piece of new lore for her.

Her father had disembarked upon Cornwall's rugged shores as a new immigrant. An indigenous Greenlander of Thule lineage, he had been driven from his homeland by Danish missionaries, accusing him of devilish witchery when his practice was more shamanistic in nature. Ingrid's mother's kin, in contrast, hailed from Myrtlewood and were sworn witches of the ancient Karrek family line. The connection must be matrilineal, she deduced.

She read aloud the passage that had caught her eye, keen on absorbing every nuance:

Each lyne of the four doth hold a fragment true,
And scripts redeem'd shall form a clew.
To unlock powers deeply stor'd,
And waken secrets Crones afford.

She mulled over the words. *Each line will have a part of the whole, and records, thus redeemed to form a key to unlocking the deeper power.* Her eyes widened, a slight shiver coursing through her at the implications of what she'd just uncovered. Four families, four elements, and now, four lines of a spell – each contributing a piece of a puzzle that could lead to unparalleled power.

Ingrid exhaled, the breath escaping her lips as a visible puff despite the warmth of the room. The subtle magic that kept her dwelling comfortable seemed to understand her mood, its aura like an empathic companion. She was both eager and apprehensive about the information she'd unearthed, and that emotion seemed to electrify the air, making her more aware of the weight of each object, the essence of each spell, and the potential of each moment.

Just then, the resonant tinkling of wind chimes and subtle bells broke her concentration. Someone – or something – was approaching her sanctuary. Her eyes snapped to the window; the chimes she'd hung from the trees were swinging, their sound a soft cacophony in the quiet.

Someone was coming.

She sighed, marking the page in the grimoire with an embroidered ribbon before closing it with a thud that seemed to echo, unbidden, around the room. Ingrid rose from her chair, placing the monocle back in its tiny, velvet-lined box. She looked towards the direction of the chimes, her expression softening for just a moment before her characteristic sternness returned.

With a sense of uneasy anticipation, she muttered, "It's about time."

CHAPTER 13
DELIA

Delia felt a deepening sense of dread as they trekked through the forest towards Ingrid's cabin. Not only was she terrified of the apparent danger from that ridiculous Order of Crimson, but also of her own volatile powers and the nameless threats that seemed to invade her dreams every night. She was also furious.

She hadn't chosen any of this; Marjie, Agatha, and Ingrid might be quite happy to plot, scheme, and mobilise, but this was their world, the magical world. Delia felt like she didn't belong.

It all seemed like a cosmic joke.

Until recently, the closest she'd come to being a witch was years ago when she'd had to duck in at the last minute in a certain unnameable Shakespearean Scottish play when an actor and their understudy had both fallen ill with the same embarrassing ailment.

As she trudged through the forest, while Marjie and Agatha bickered both playfully and grumpily, Delia felt the urge to run.

Perhaps London wasn't safe right now for her, but there was no reason for her to stay here. On the other hand, a stroppy voice inside her kept insisting that the show must go on. She was made of stronger stuff than this.

And what was a life without magic, now that she knew magic existed?

Smoke was puffing cheerfully from the chimney as they arrived at the cabin. The door swung open for them, though Ingrid was nowhere in sight.

Marjie and Agatha entered, taking seats by the fire, while Delia lingered near the door, torn between facing her fears or running away like some annoying character in a play, not ready to face her destiny.

The realisation that Delia couldn't live with being a coward turned her attention back towards facing her fears. She took a deep breath and stepped into the hut.

"You might want a little of this calming tonic, dear," Marjie suggested, fishing out a bottle from her bag and passing it to Delia.

"Good idea," Ingrid added, entering through the back door. "I don't want you accidentally setting my house on fire. That would be terribly rude."

Marjie agreed.

"Fine," said Delia, accepting the bottle of tonic.

"The tea is brewed," said Ingrid, instead of welcoming them.

Moments later, a teapot began pouring tea of its own accord and cups were flying around the room to their respective visitors.

"Right, let's get down to business," said Ingrid.

"You haven't spiked this with anything?" Delia asked, sniffing the cup.

"It's just chamomile and peppermint, I'm afraid," said Ingrid. "I save the magic mushrooms for special occasions."

"Maybe I can have some of that?" Agatha nodded towards the bottle that Delia was still holding.

"I can get you some if you really must have it," Marjie responded. "But that one's for Delia."

Agatha rolled her eyes.

Delia added a few drops of the potion into her tea. She trusted Marjie more than most others in the room, and likely more than most people in general. There was something so warm and genuinely kind about her.

After a sip of the tea, Delia's shoulders relaxed, and she felt a sensation she wasn't used to. It took her a moment to identify it as gratitude – appreciation for being here with these new, if odd, friends, and a newfound awe bloomed in her chest, a wondering thankfulness for the magic of her own life.

"This is good stuff," she said, passing the bottle to Agatha. "Try some if you like."

Marjie shook her head and Agatha scowled. "Why don't I get to have any fun?"

"This one's especially for you, Delia. I made it with your

energy in mind," Marjie replied. "You know you can come to me anytime, Aggie."

"Don't call me that," Agatha snapped.

Marjie squinted at her. "You told us to call you that when you were drunk last time."

"Well, don't call me that unless I'm drunk," Agatha corrected herself. "Speaking of drunk...Do you have any sherry?"

"No. Someone's drunk me dry, I'm afraid," said Ingrid wryly.

Agatha huffed.

"Besides," Ingrid continued, "I didn't invite you here for some kind of drinking bender. I said 'let's get down to business', and I meant it." She unfurled a scroll that looked like parchment, letting it roll out onto the table. "Gather 'round."

They sat around, peering at the fresh ink, including scrawled writing and diagrams that Delia didn't understand. "What is all this?" she asked.

"Based on the book, I'm mapping out what we need to do at the solstice," Ingrid explained.

"Ah, this is Myrtlewood," said Marjie, pointing at the map. "This is the centre of town."

"So it is," said Delia, although it wasn't exactly what she would call an accurate depiction.

"Winter solstice is celebrated here." Ingrid pointed to a circle in the middle of the supposed map.

"And it's quite the party!" said Agatha.

Ingrid frowned. "According to the book, the winter solstice is the most auspicious time to unlock the second stage of crone power. Based on my research it's clear to me that after the ritual we've got to make our way through the forest over here to find *something* in the woods."

"The book talks about Myrtlewood?" Delia asked.

"Of course it does," Ingrid replied. "What we're discussing here is the ancestral magic of the town. The four Elemental Crones of Myrtlewood are tied to this land, to its history."

"Then why wasn't the book here?" Delia wondered aloud.

Ingrid furrowed her brow. "These are ancient and powerful magics. We may never know the exact reasoning, however I believe the book was taken and hidden very deliberately in that poor old town."

"Are you suggesting it the book is the reason the hamlet of Gildea was destroyed?" Marjie asked.

"I suspect so," Agatha chimed in. "Though that was long ago."

"Fortunately," Ingrid continued, "the book was so well-protected that whoever came after it wasn't able to reach it."

Delia shuddered. "I wouldn't be surprised if that was the Order of Crimson – they seem zealous enough to destroy a whole settlement just to get their hands on power. I'm glad they didn't get it then, and that we managed to evade them, but now that the protective magic has been released and we have the book, surely we've in far greater danger."

"Not while the invisibility magic still holds," Marjie reassured her. "I have utmost faith in whoever went to such great lengths to protect the crone power. Presumably it was an earlier generation of crones."

Agatha nodded. "A plan well-executed is a rare thing indeed. It seems rather a lot of thought has gone into protecting that wee tome." She gestured over to the book which Delia thought was rather large and not 'wee' at all, however she sensed Agatha was referring to the grimoire in that way as a term of endearment and she couldn't help but smile at that thought.

"This path here," said Marjie, tracing her finger along Ingrid's map, "goes rather close to your house, doesn't it, Ingrid?"

Delia peered at the map again, wondering how Marjie was figuring all this out when the scrawling seemed utterly mysterious to her.

Ingrid crossed her arms. "What of it?"

Marjie shrugged. "I don't know. It's just an interesting coincidence. I mean, if there was something I was trying to find and it was close to my house, I would feel..."

"You would feel what?" Ingrid asked.

"Like perhaps you should know more about it than you do," Agatha finished bluntly.

"I can't tell whether you're being suspicious of me, or just unimpressed with my lack of knowledge of ancient mysteries that have been buried for at least a century," Ingrid said, her voice laced with stony irony.

"Why not both?" said Agatha wryly.

"Look, this hardly seems the time to be bickering about who

should or shouldn't know things," Delia interjected. "To be quite frank, there's nothing I'd like more than to escape this whole drama."

Agatha sighed. "Let me guess, you're feeling like you didn't sign up for this. It's not fair. You're scared, and you're angry. You want to run off, but you're too stubborn to actually do it."

Delia scowled at her. "That about covers it," she admitted.

"Good, I'm glad you've had Marjie's tonic," said Ingrid.

"Is that because you're about to double-cross us or because you don't want me setting you on fire?" Delia asked.

"The latter," Ingrid said. "I guarantee that your fears and your rage are only going to get more intense as your powers grow and you haven't yet mastered even the basics of them."

"That's another thing that's infuriating," said Delia, folding her arms. Then she felt heat rush through her hands as smoke began to rise from her chest. She quickly released her arms, shaking her hands in the air, trying to calm down.

Agatha cackled. "Smoking's bad for your health, you know."

"More tea, dear," Marjie suggested warmly.

"Right," said Delia, taking a big gulp.

"Look, we don't expect you to have mastered your powers yet," Ingrid reassured her. "And I don't think any of us really have, to be quite candid."

"Speak for yourself," Agatha protested.

They all gave her an unimpressed look. "What? I'm a witch through and through."

"As am I," said Ingrid. "And Marjie too. However, the

73

elemental power of the crones is more than any normal witch should ever have to handle in their lives. As much as it's a blessing, it's also a burden. Until you can summon a cyclone, Agatha, or command the tides, Marjie, or until I can actually get the earth to move, we have not mastered or even properly unleashed our powers. I'm just saying this to humble us all."

"Glad you're not just trying to make me feel better," said Delia. "Then I'd have to be more suspicious of you."

Ingrid chuckled.

"We do have another small problem," said Marjie. "I might be double booked for the night of the winter solstice."

"You're joking," said Ingrid.

Agatha shook her head slowly. "I'm afraid she isn't. Those Thorn girls have gotten themselves in a pickle again. And the winter solstice is important for them."

"That about sums it up," said Marjie. "I can't just abandon Rosemary and Athena when they need me. They're trying to get to the underworld."

Ingrid spluttered on her tea and then began coughing wildly. "Outrageous," she exclaimed. "I know those witches are powerful. Everyone knows it. But the underworld is not a place you go."

"Be that as it may," said Marjie. "I have a feeling that they're going to need me that night. Which does put us in rather a pickle, as Agatha said."

"Unlocking the power of the Crones is more important than helping your friends," Ingrid reasoned. "Besides, if they're getting themselves into trouble, they should get themselves out of it."

"Well, that's all very well to say," argued Marjie, "but they're more than friends. They're my family. My chosen family, anyway. I don't want to back out and leave you in the lurch."

"You can't," said Ingrid. "We need you."

Marjie sighed. "All I'm saying is, I have to balance my commitments."

"Well, perhaps you can do both," Delia suggested. "I mean, if everyone's going to the winter solstice celebrations, that's where the energy is. Then why not multitask? We can all share the load and help watch out for Rosemary and Athena. While we also do whatever croning we need to do. Besides, if the Order manage to break through the magical protections by then, they're bound to try and attack on solstice night. It's an obvious time, isn't it? And there'll be strength in numbers if we're all there together."

Marjie smiled. "I hope you're right, dear. I'd hate to let anyone down."

Ingrid gave Delia an impressed look. "Sounds like we've got ourselves a plan," she said.

"Maybe even a new leader," Agatha muttered.

"We don't have leaders," Ingrid protested.

"That's just what a leader would say," Agatha teased. "Also, the leader is probably the scariest one."

"What are you implying?" Ingrid asked, her mouth curling into a small smile.

"Well," said Agatha, taking a swig of her tea, "you might be a terrifying forest witch, but Delia is probably the most dangerous among us."

"Careful," warned Delia, "you might find yourself rather charred if you continue on like that."

Ingrid shook her head. "None of you are brave enough to attack me in my own house, especially not when an ancient and powerful book is sitting right there. Oh, that reminds me. It seems we all need to find our old family grimoires, apparently they'll all reveal something, which when we piece it together will be of some use to us in the final stages of unlocking the ancient Elemental Crone magic."

"Our what?" Delia asked.

"Each witching family has a special grimoire," Agatha explained. "Passed down through the generations."

"Err, but I don't even know my magical family, so that's currently impossible," Delia pointed out.

Marjie looked down at the floor, and her shoulders slumped.

"Well, you'll just have to find out—"

Agatha was interrupted as the door creaked open and the cat Mephistos sauntered in.

"I see you're having a meeting without me," he said, hopping up on the table and looking unimpressed.

"We can't wait around for you all day," said Ingrid.

"What's this?" asked Mephistos in a bored voice, pointing at the map.

"It's a secret," said Ingrid.

"Seems fairly obvious to me," he remarked. "Although, I'd

advise against going into cartography. You don't have the attention to detail for it."

Ingrid scowled at him. "If you're just here to insult us—"

"No, I'm here with news," Mephistos purred. "For your information, I have been spying on the Order of Crimson. They have an encampment just past the edge of the forest," he said. "They're plotting something for winter solstice."

"But they can't see us, can they?" said Delia.

"No," the cat replied. "They seem to think that there's a way of magically unlocking your cloaking so that they can carry on with their mission."

Ingrid scoffed. "We could have guessed about the winter solstice, so you're not bringing us any new information. But thanks for the effort. Anything else?"

Mephistos regarded her with a level of arrogant scorn only possible from a cat. "Well, they keep going on about dragons..."

Ingrid shuddered and shook her head.

"What are they saying about dragons?" Delia asked.

Mephistos turned towards her and his eyes gleamed. "They're going to try and harness the power of dragons to restore the world to its rightful order."

Delia frowned. "But what does that mean?"

Ingrid scoffed again. "Knowing those ridiculous old fogies, it will be something like the Middle Ages. Their version of a church will be in control and women will be powerless."

"We can't let them do it, you know," said Agatha. "We must

destroy the dragons. That's what the Crones are supposed to do, isn't it?"

Delia shook her head. Dragons were supposedly horrendously powerful and terrifying beasts, but still, destroying them seemed wrong. "Well, I'm not sure we're in any fit state to—"

"We will be after the solstice," Ingrid insisted.

"That's the spirit, dear," Marjie added, taking a big gulp of Delia's tea.

CHAPTER 14
THE SHEPERD

F ather Benedict paced in his meticulously organised strategy room. The rows of scrolls had been aligned in impeccable order, and the maps stretched out on the oak table were held taut with military precision. Every quill in its ink pot, every candle flame —frozen in stasis – echoed a sanctum of control, a bulwark against the chaotic forces he so loathed.

His jaw clenched, Father Benedict scowled as he scanned the reports from various operatives, not satisfied with the lack of progress in locating the elusive crones.

Just as he was about to turn his attention to another stack of scrolls, the door creaked open.

"Did I summon you?" Father Benedict snapped at the Cleric who timidly entered the room, a scroll clutched in his hand.

"I bring news, Shepherd," the Cleric stammered, his voice tinged with both urgency and hesitance.

Father Benedict looked down at the man disapprovingly, waiting until the Cleric bowed his head in reverence before tersely commanding him, "Proceed."

"The surveillance team has submitted a report from London – concerning the fire witch's apartment," said the Cleric, unfurling the scroll. "It seems a woman has been visiting the premises."

Father Benedict's eyes narrowed, his fists trembling in suppressed rage. "Why was this not immediately relayed to me?"

"The team thought it was irrelevant, Shepherd," the Cleric stammered. "The woman knocked on the door, swore loudly, and left, both times. It was assumed she hadn't been informed of the fire witch's whereabouts. They made a note that she might be a debt collector of some sort."

Father Benedict inhaled sharply, containing his anger. "Describe this woman."

Reading from the scroll, the Cleric said, "She is tall, appears to be in her fifties or sixties, though hard to determine due to the heavy makeup. She has black and blonde streaked hair cut short in the style that I believe is colloquially termed 'a bob'."

A malicious gleam flared in the Shepherd's eyes. "Prepare a dossier on this woman immediately for the special team."

"Team?"

"Yes, you must assemble one forthwith. Pick some of the members who understand the outside world best. We may have just discovered a thread we can pull."

The Cleric's eyes widened, hesitant. "But, Shepherd—"

"Do as you are commanded!" Father Benedict barked, cutting him off.

The Cleric swallowed his reservations and scurried out of the room, leaving Father Benedict to return to his thoughts and a rare thrill of satisfaction. For the first time in a while, chaos had presented him an opportunity he hadn't yet considered. He knew this Mission inside and out. He had studied, researched, and shaped its path for decades, and the woman the Cleric mentioned was another piece of the puzzle. It was a small crack in the edifice that protected the Myrtlewood Crones, but it was a crack nonetheless.

Father Benedict clasped his hands behind his back, resolute. He looked again at the rows of scrolls, the painstakingly detailed maps, and the silent candle flames. They seemed to whisper back at him, a silent chorus confirming his newfound belief.

Order would prevail. It was only a matter of time.

CHAPTER 15
DELIA

The midwinter sun shone through the clouds. Delia was dressed up warmly in her coat, which Marjie had kindly magically altered with a charm to protect her from chills. So even though the icy air touched her face, she felt toasty and warm as she left the house, made her way down the snowy path, and out towards the village.

The little beagle puppy she sometimes saw around Myrtlewood barked and ran up to her for a pat.

"Hello, you sweet wee fellow," said Delia, scratching him behind the ears. "Where do you even live? Who do you belong to?"

The puppy gave a happy yap and turned around in a circle before running off.

Delia didn't dawdle; today she had a mission of her own.

Ingrid had made it clear that in order to unlock the full potential of Crone magic, there were at least two more stages: one was linked to the night of the winter solstice, and the other required locating each grimoire from the families of each of the four crones, including her own.

The problem was, Delia knew nothing of her magical heritage, aside from awareness that her grandmother had been associated with Myrtlewood. Ingrid perhaps knew more, but whatever she knew, she wasn't saying.

It didn't take Delia long to get to the municipal buildings of the village. Being a tiny town as it was, the building was not large and grand. However, it did have a stately appearance, with Ionic pillars at the front.

She pushed her way in through the double doors to find that the front counter of the building was unstaffed.

A tiny domed bell sat there, and Delia waited a moment before ringing it.

"You called?" said a voice, rather abruptly.

A man appeared, though Delia wasn't quite sure where he came from. It took her a moment to realise that the eccentric fellow in front of her, in the velvet purple robe, was Ferg, the mayor, who she'd met briefly when she'd first arrived in Myrtlewood.

"Oh, hello. I was just looking for someone to show me to the records," Delia said.

"The records?" Ferg raised an eyebrow.

"Yes," Delia replied. "I don't want to take up your time. I'm sure you've got more important things to do."

He eyed her quizzically.

"You're Delia Spark," Ferg replied.

"I can wait for someone else to help me out." Delia looked around.

"I'm afraid nobody else is here. In fact, for some reason, I have trouble keeping employees." Ferg looked down at his nails. "None of them are quite up to standard."

"Oh...I wonder why," said Delia, trying to keep her voice casual and not sarcastic. After all, she did really want to see those records.

"What records are you looking for?" Ferg asked, narrowing his eyes.

"The records of the town, naturally," said Delia. "I'm trying to get information about my grandmother who may have lived here at some point."

Ferg waited for a moment, almost as if the silence he presented was some sort of test. Delia knew how to negotiate, so instead of rambling on or trying to push ahead, she merely stood there and allowed a subtle confident smile to stretch across her lips.

Ferg took a deep breath and then dramatically exhaled. "Right, this way!" He gestured with dramatic flair and led Delia through a corridor and then down some stairs to a rather large underground room populated with old, musty bookshelves.

The area was lit with torches, affixed to the walls, which ignited upon their entry.

"I should have expected something like this, I suppose," Delia muttered.

"What do you mean?" Ferg asked. "Isn't everything in order?"

"Oh, you know, the torches – the massive shelves of old tomes..."

"Of course," said Ferg, frowning in confusion. "And what records are you looking for?"

"Like I said, I'm looking for anything about my ancestors, the Spark family."

Ferg nodded with a knowing look. "The Sparks..."

"Yes, my grandmother was a Spark. Her name was Etty."

"A legend in her own right," said Ferg.

Delia sighed. "Nobody tells me a thing about her."

"People sometimes have a rather short memory around here. And besides, there was all that business with a fire...or so I've read, it was before my time," Ferg mused.

"Yes, the fire," said Delia, looking down at her hands. Did she have the same power that her grandmother had? That would make sense, but the way Ferg had said it sounded more sinister. As far as Delia knew, her grandmother had died from emphysema after decades of smoking, yet the way everyone was acting suggested something devious had happened.

"Right this way," said Ferg, gesturing for her to follow him down a long aisle filled with old tomes. "I suspect everything that you're looking for will be on this shelf." The bookcase was labelled with a large 'S'.

"Spark..." Ferg ran his hand along the spines of several large volumes before pulling one out and handing it to her.

"Can I take it?" asked Delia.

"Of course not," said Ferg. "What kind of records collection would this be if I just let people wander off with them?"

"Oh," said Delia, looking at the floor like a child getting a telling off from a grumpy librarian.

"However, you may peruse it." He gestured over to the side of the room where a small table and chair were propped up beside one of the flaming torches.

"All right," said Delia, trying to smile. "Thank you. I might be some time. You can go about your business."

"I will," said Ferg replied, but did not move.

"Is there anything else?" she asked him, although she felt like he should be the one asking her that.

"We need you for the theatre troupe," Ferg blurted out.

"Oh...I can't," said Delia. "I'm sorry, I've retired."

Shame and anguish washed over her for a moment; a past memory that she'd long been suppressing emerged. A dark stage. A spotlight. A big moment. A snapping heel—

Delia shook herself. The thought of working in a small-town theatre troupe was a kind of embarrassment in itself, considering the lofty heights of her career. But for some reason, an old wound had surfaced. Perhaps even the thought of the theatre at all was painful for her at this moment.

"I don't need an answer straight away," said Ferg. "However, come along to the Winter Solstice. You'll see us perform, and you can tell me what you think."

Delia blinked at him.

"Be brutal," he said with such a serious tone that Delia almost burst out laughing.

"I will be at the Winter Solstice," Delia admitted.

"Excellent," said Ferg, tapping his fingertips together. "I will leave you to peruse."

He vanished rather quickly, though not by magic, and Delia carried the heavy book over to the table and opened it.

The first section of the book was hard to decipher. There was rather a lot of cursive scroll; it was tiny and illegible, even with her reading glasses. It seemed to be written in a language that she didn't understand. However, as she flicked through, things became clearer. It seemed there was rather a long line of Sparks in Myrtlewood, connecting with several other families, the names of which she didn't recognise.

She skipped right to the end, wondering how far the records and the genealogy went, only to see her grandmother's name.

Ettalina Spark.

It ended there. And Delia felt an odd pang of loss. Nobody had recorded her or her parents here; it was as if the line had ended with her grandmother.

Perhaps that would have been the case, magically at least, if she hadn't had her rather late-in-life magical awakening along with the power of the crones.

More interesting still was that the family line went on from a different branch. "She had a sister…" Delia muttered to herself. "Thero Bracewell. Funny name…"

She couldn't think of any Bracewells, but the name tasted almost metallic on her tongue. She felt a kind of zinging energy.

Delia took a sharp inhale of breath realising the implications: it was a whole family tree meaning she had a whole family of cousins, some of whom were probably still living.

She ran her hand over the names. They all sounded rather odd and old-fashioned, but she supposed that should not be surprising; they were likely from a different era, much like her grandmother and apparently this whole village.

A strange sensation passed through her body, almost like the throes of a fever. Delia had a whole family that she knew nothing of. Would they want to meet her? Would they have the grimoire?

Delia's parents were long gone. She'd thought she had no family other than Gillian, Merryn, and Keyne; they had been so distant from her recently – an ache that she had to continue to suppress because it was too painful. Although Gilly had promised to come at Christmas and bring the kids with her which was some consolation. The wait was probably wise. Delia gathered that it would be far too dangerous to see them before the winter solstice.

Delia took her phone out of her pocket and snapped a few images of the most recent parts of the family tree.

She heaved the heavy book closed and did her best to return it to the shelf where she thought Ferg had pulled it out from.

Something had changed; she knew it instinctively, yet she couldn't quite put a finger on what it was. Delia began to make her way back down the corridor, a growing dread weighing her down.

CHAPTER 16

MARJIE

Marjie pushed open the front door of Thorn Manor, her body trembling slightly as if she'd burst through a spiderweb of unspoken fears and memories.

The kitchen was empty, lit only by the late afternoon sun filtering through stained-glass windows that cast ethereal patterns on the wooden floor.

She guessed that Rosemary and Athena were either out or sleeping – those two had been keeping the strangest hours since they started collaborating with the Dreamweaver in the Southern Hemisphere.

She filled the kettle and set it on the stove. The hum of the boiling water seemed to emphasise the loneliness of the house – a house full of magic, and yet devoid of the immediate comfort of family.

Ingrid's revelation about each Crone needing to find their

old family grimoires to unlock the final level of crone magic had unsettled Marjie more than she'd admitted.

For years, she'd shoved away thoughts of her estranged family like old photographs in a dusty attic.

Now, it seemed, the past would have to be unpacked.

The matter of her own family grimoire was a subject she'd managed to avoid for years but could no longer.

She could feel the weight of that old leather-bound book, its pages filled with spells and wisdom passed down through generations, even though it was miles away, both in distance and in emotional terrain.

Her hands shaking as she prepared a pot of tea, then, remembering that she had a new blend to test, she put the kettle back on to boil. She tacked the brewing teapot on a tray with a plate of orange and currant biscuits and carried it into the living room to enjoy afternoon tea.

As if sensing her mood, the hearth burst into a comforting fire.

The flames danced and flickered, a choreographed ballet of heat and light. Marjie sank into the plush chair beside it and sighed.

Thorn Manor was an old friend, and in that moment, she felt its warm embrace envelop her. It was good to feel cared for, even by a sentient home.

Papa Jack also had that comforting effect on her, but she had to keep her distance. There were too many secrets she couldn't share with him – no one else could know about the Crone magic.

Marjie couldn't even tell Rosemary and Athena about it, but then again, they had enough on their plates.

The problem was, Marjie needed to talk to someone. Perhaps Delia would understand. The poor woman was navigating her own tricky familial situation, with no clue about her magical heritage or who she was in a world where lineage seemed to matter so much.

Marjie hadn't spoken to her family in so many years. The thought of her estrangement was a gnawing source of shame. Even Rosemary, who had become like a daughter to her, was oblivious to this hidden corner of Marjie's life.

Marjie's fingers traced the rim of her tea cup as she contemplated her next move. Should she pick up the phone and dial the number that she had written down but never dared to call? What would her brother even say? And if by some small miracle, he had the grimoire, would he be willing to share it?

Too many questions and not enough courage.

Marjie sighed again. The walls of Thorn Manor seemed to sigh with her, as if sharing in her emotional turmoil. Perhaps it was time to brave the uncharted waters of her past. After all, if the fate of the town and possibly the world was hanging in the balance, then surely, she could at least attempt to mend a personal rift. She couldn't expect to heal the world if she couldn't even heal her own family.

As she sat there, a part of her yearned for the power just to reach into those old, dusty corners of her life and pull out the grimoire that might hold the keys to their future. And as much as she hesitated, she knew, deep down, that some doors needed to be reopened, no matter how firmly they had been shut.

With a sigh that was a complex brew of determination and resignation, Marjie decided that it was finally time to make that call. Whatever the outcome, the fate of Myrtlewood, and possibly much more, hung delicately in the balance. And if the Myrtlewood Crones were at the heart of this tapestry of fate, then she had her own threads to contribute, no matter how tangled they might be.

The kettle in the kitchen whistled again, as if nudging her into action.

Taking a deep breath, Marjie made a resolve. Tomorrow, she'd make the call. For now, she'd sip her tea, brew some more, and let Thorn Manor's magic cocoon her, giving her the strength she'd need for the challenges that lay ahead.

CHAPTER 17
DELIA

As Delia made her way back out through the reception of the municipal building, a series of odd-sounding names churned in her head.

Family names.

Family.

She had a whole lot of cousins she'd never even heard of and she didn't even know how to pronounce their names.

"Life is full of surprises," she muttered to herself, then she froze.

Someone was sitting at the front desk and it wasn't Ferg.

A woman with dark, straight hair, tinted purple, sat there wearing a plum pinstripe suit. She turned to look at Delia. "Can I help you?"

Delia shook her head. "No, I was just...I thought nobody else worked here. Ferg, the mayor, said he had trouble keeping staff."

The woman chuckled. "I'm not staff; I'm a contractor. I just pop in from time to time between other jobs to do a few things for his Lordship, or whatever he calls himself now."

"Quite a character, isn't he," said Delia, smiling at the younger woman and admiring her bold style.

"He's better than the last mayor, I have to say."

Delia pursed her lips. "Not sure what that says about this town."

"I'm Juniper," said the woman with a smile, holding out her hand. Delia shook it.

"Delia." She completed the handshake. "And I'm new here. I was just looking at records."

"Oh yes," said Juniper with mild interest. "Anything in particular?"

"Just my own family history. It turns out I know nothing about it."

"Your family's from Myrtlewood?" Juniper asked, sounding interested.

"Apparently so. My grandmother was. It turns out she had all this other family, and I need to somehow get hold of them and locate an old family grimoire. It's quite important."

Delia wasn't quite sure why she was saying all this to a stranger, but nothing she said was secret, or gave away particular details about the crones.

"Fascinating," Juniper replied. "I love a good mystery."

Delia's eyes narrowed as she looked at Juniper. She seemed

to have her head screwed on; she was probably in her forties and seemed sharp enough.

"You're a contractor," Delia ventured. "Do you happen to take on private investigations?"

"On occasion," Juniper replied. "I basically do whatever kinds of work need to be done in the magical world. Nothing too sinister, though."

"Glad to hear it," said Delia with a nervous laugh.

"You want me to try and track down your family for you?"

Delia sighed. "I don't know...I suppose I have to do it somehow."

"Any names?"

Delia pulled out her phone. "You don't happen to know the Bracewell family, do you?"

Juniper coughed; it almost seemed as though she was choking.

"Are you quite alright?" Delia asked her.

"Oh yes. It's just, well, the Bracewell family...you might say, is notorious."

Delia grimaced. "That does not bode well."

"They're one of the most ruthless, power-crazed families I've ever heard of."

Delia braced herself against a sinking sensation. "I don't suppose they're likely to lend me the grimoire, then?"

Juniper gave her a nervous smile. "I'd say your chances are fairly slim."

"Then perhaps I do need a professional." Delia fished around in her wallet for a card; it was a theatre business card with her old surname, but it did have her mobile number on it. "If you happen to have the time with all your other work, perhaps you could dig up some information for me on them?"

"I might be able to help you with that," Juniper said, taking the card. "Any information in particular?"

Delia waved her hand vaguely. "I just need to know anything that will be useful. I suppose I need to get to know them, make friends with them somehow, if I'm going to get a chance at even taking a peek at their grimoire."

"You say 'their grimoire'," said Juniper, tucking the card away and folding her arms, "but if it's really an ancient family grimoire, it's yours too."

Delia gave her a tight-lipped smile. "Don't suppose the Bracewells will share that opinion."

"Probably not," Juniper conceded. "See, you know them already."

Delia laughed.

"I've got a few things to carry on with," said Juniper, "but here's my card." She handed over a small rectangle of board, the same shade as her hair and suit. "Give me a call if you have any questions."

Delia thanked her and stowed the card in her bag. She turned back to say goodbye, only to see the woman in front of her disappear into thin air.

Delia shook her head. "I'm not sure if I'm ever going to get used to this place," she muttered, and promptly left the building.

CHAPTER 18

THE ROGUE

Declan sat in a secluded part of the forest, away from prying eyes. The flickering light from the campfire danced across his rugged face, casting shadows that mirrored his fragmented thoughts.

The aroma of the game he'd hunted earlier mingled with the earthy scent of foraged rosemary, thyme, wild garlic, and edible mushrooms that only revealed themselves to those who knew where to look. Even as he picked at his meal, his mind flexed and stretched against trying contradictions.

Over time, many things may change in the human world, but the essence of nature remained. The same plants had grown in this forest a thousand years ago, offering themselves to foragers like him.

It was comforting but also highlighted a painful contradiction about humanity's evolving relationship with nature. Less and less sense, less respect, and certainly less wisdom seemed to prevail among humans as their technology and supposed intellect developed.

Despite their constant evolution, people held less respect for the natural world. They expanded their cities, swallowed up the woodlands.

Before long, there'd be nothing left. Not unless things changed dramatically.

He chewed on a piece of game, its juices mingling with the foraged herbs, and pondered this painful paradox.

The Order of Crimson had been oddly silent. On occasion, Declan had journeyed to the outskirts of Myrtlewood. It was there, just beyond its boundaries, that he could receive their cryptic messages. Declan assumed they were still in chaos. The Order were still looking for a way through the powerful invisibility magic that shrouded the town. They assumed he was doing the same.

Declan couldn't afford to be seen within the Myrtlewood village; the mere sight of him would send Delia and the other Crones into high alert. So he kept to his hidden camp, amidst the tall trees whose branches swayed like ancient sages whispering secrets. It was a sanctuary from obligations, contracts, and an Order whose motives remained as murky as a moonless night.

Yes, the Order seemed to be in disarray, but Declan couldn't shake the feeling that even this mess was calculated. Someone was pulling the strings.

Declan was no puppet. He refused to become one, but he

wanted to understand the Order. From what he could gather from them, and from the whispered rumours about them, they appeared to want a return to a time where men held dominion, a world Declan had lived through many times before and knew well there was nothing noble about it.

His hands tightened around a wooden spoon carved from a fallen branch, its coarse texture grounding him momentarily.

Never mind what the Order wanted, what did *he* even want anymore? Declan's emotions, once dulled by time, were awakening in new, unsettling ways. The situation in Myrtlewood, the power the Crones wielded, it was compelling in a way nothing had been for a long time.

His instincts twitched, sending a shiver up his spine. Something dangerous was approaching. His mind circled back to the Order but quickly dismissed the thought; the Order couldn't penetrate Myrtlewood's magical boundaries, and this threat felt as if it was from another plane altogether.

Reaching into his rucksack, his fingers found the cold, smooth surface of his seer's stone.

Declan closed his eyes and murmured an incantation older than the trees surrounding him. His mind plunged into a trance, deepening until he felt his consciousness detach from his physical body.

In this state, he floated upwards, seeing into a deeper layer of the land: its ethereal imprints.

Ascending over the town, on this etheric plane, he sensed a presence. Pure malevolence.

Destructive chaos.

And there it was – a dark shadow hovering above the town. As soon as he sensed it, the entity became aware of his watchful eye.

It vanished, leaving Declan unsettled in a way he hadn't felt in centuries.

Declan's eyes snapped open to reveal his campfire. His awareness was firmly back in his body back in the tangible world, but what he'd felt left an indelible mark.

Declan pondered upon the newfound threat. The Order, with all their misguided quests, paled in comparison. This destructive entity was an unknown variable, and in its shadow, the Order's agenda seemed a lesser evil.

It left Declan pondering the changing dynamics of his existence. Only a month ago, he wouldn't have cared about any of this. But now, as he sat there with the aroma of cooked game filling the air, he found himself reluctantly acknowledging that he did.

The revelation was unsettling.

Sweat trickled down his temple, the fire's heat suddenly suffocating.

Few things had disturbed him in recent centuries, but this did. He knew with gut-wrenching certainty that a powerful malevolent force was lurking nearby, perhaps waiting for an opening, an opportunity to strike and cause catastrophe.

His gaze returned to the fire, watching the flames dance and contort as if mimicking the chaos that loomed. He leaned back against a tree, its bark rough against his skin, grounding him in its ancient, unchanging reality. But even as he sat there, senses honed, instincts on alert, he understood that the game had changed, and he, the eternal rogue, was racing to keep up with his own unfolding enigma.

CHAPTER 19
DELIA

The winter sunlight warmed her face pleasantly as Delia sat at the kitchen table nursing a well-deserved second coffee of the morning after at least an hour of trying and failing to control her firepower.

Her attempts had led to setting various parts of the garden on fire. It was still astonishing to her that snow could burn!

Suffice to say, she was yet to master the control she was aiming for.

She'd mistakenly thought it would be simple. After all, they'd done so much work to release the crone powers. However, Ingrid and Agatha had carefully explained that the entire adventure to retrieve the special book and cast the invisibility spell which had protected them from the Order, had only been the first stage of a process.

The magic, it seemed, had been very carefully concealed so

that it could only be accessed and utilised, if and when needed, by those who were both called to it and capable of wielding it.

Delia currently wasn't capable of wielding her own powers. She very much doubted whether she would be qualified for whatever the full crone powers entailed. However, she was determined to try.

It had seemed so easy back when she'd set that cowboy's hat on fire. It had been so satisfying too. That had been controlled.

Unfortunately it seemed that under less adrenaline-inducing circumstances, such as standing in the garden of her house, she couldn't seem to master it.

Nine attempts out of ten, she got nothing at all. No flames, no fire, not even hot steam. The rest of the time she produced the kind of inferno that one would only deliberately unleash on the very rare occasions when it couldn't do devastating damage. Generally, that kind of fire power was far more trouble than it was worth.

Delia sighed, but she didn't beat herself up. She took another sip of coffee, gave herself a little pep talk, and promised to try again tomorrow.

Just then, the doorbell rang. She looked around the room as if to question who might be popping by. Of course, there was nobody to ask. In that moment of obvious emptiness, Delia had never felt so alone. However, her loneliness quickly evaporated when she answered the door to find Marjie standing there.

Marjie immediately enveloped Delia in a warm hug while brandishing a paper bag filled with delicious-smelling baking.

Delia invited Marjie in and made her some tea; the only appropriate thing to do in such a situation.

Delia took a bite of the mouth-watering leek and mustard pasty that Marjie had delivered to her.

"This is outstanding," Delia said, with a small groan of pleasure.

Marjie beamed at her, but as her smile faded, Delia noticed sadness in her eyes.

"What's wrong?" Delia asked.

"Oh, nothing, dear."

"It doesn't look like nothing," Delia said matter-of-factly.

Marjie sniffed slightly, and Delia wondered if Marjie was doing a good job of hiding the fact that she had cried recently.

"Marjie?" Delia said.

Marjie sighed. "I suppose it's safe to tell you. I've just never talked about this with anyone, you see. Not even Rosemary. It's not that I wouldn't share it with her; I just wouldn't want to burden her. Especially not now with the winter solstice and everything."

"Burden her with what?" Delia asked, crossing her arms. "I'm sure no matter what you say, it won't be a burden to me. Especially not considering how wonderfully welcoming you've been to me. And I'm not just talking about the baking. I already consider you to be a good friend. And that's a rare thing for me, you know; I've only really had one good friend until recently."

The corner of Marjie's mouth twitched. "Alright, then. I

suppose I can tell you about it. It's just...Ingrid's talk of what she read in that crusty old book."

Delia giggled. "You mean the grimoire?"

"I've got a bone to pick with that thing," said Marjie.

"It's something about your family?" Delia guessed.

"How did you know?" Marjie looked shocked.

Delia shrugged. "Well, Ingrid and Agatha seem to have their family grimoires, whereas you and I do not. I have only just begun figuring out who my family might be. You've been relatively silent on the topic. Am I guessing correctly that perhaps all is not well when it comes to your family of origin?"

"You could say that," said Marjie. "It's a bit of a tragic story, though. I don't tend to talk about it."

"Well, let's change that," said Delia. "A problem shared is a problem halved, and all that. Besides, I've got enough family dysfunctions; I'm hardly going to be judgmental, am I?"

"Our family problems are somewhat old ones," said Marjie. "You see, when I was growing up, a terrible thing happened. My sweet younger brother, Jowell, was tragically killed by a werewolf."

"Oh," Delia gulped. "Werewolves do exist?"

"Yes," said Marjie. "I held such a grudge for many years about werewolves. I've done a lot of processing on that recently, partly because of Rosemary's encouragement. But my main problem isn't the werewolves themselves. You see, after sweet Jowell died, my parents were so bereft with grief that they shut down."

"I couldn't imagine losing a child," said Delia, uttering a silent prayer that Gillian was alright. She'd responded to messages recently, and they'd had a few brief phone calls. Gilly had remained distant, but she seemed to be getting on okay. Delia turned her attention back to Marjie. "It must have been awful, for all of you."

"My parents withdrew," Marjie continued. "And my older brother, Graham, well, he didn't take the situation well at all. You see, he decided that it wasn't just werewolves and magical creatures; it was the entire magical world to blame for not protecting us adequately. He partly blamed my parents, I think, though they were no great magical practitioners themselves. My mother was an expert at domestic magic, and my father, well, he was a shopkeeper. But he was a rather talented witch. My father came from a very old witching family. I suspect that it's the lineage that makes me eligible to be a crone. His family had been in Myrtlewood for such a long time, whereas my mother had come over from Bermuda as a young woman. She was a servant to a wealthy family and she was of African descent. That's where I get my lovely complexion." Marjie twinkled. "I think of her often when I'm in the kitchen, especially when I'm in the mood for some of her famous rum cake."

Delia smiled warmly back at her, but Marjie's expression quickly returned to one of sadness.

"Anyway," Marjie continued. "My parents were so affected by the tragedy and Graham just seemed to blame everyone for it, including my father who'd been in the shop at the time. Jowell was only eleven; he'd gone wandering off into the forest alone. I was thirteen and my older brother was sixteen and we'd been at home that day. I had always had more magical fortitude than Graham. He was never very good at spell work, though he excelled at other things at school."

"I see," said Delia. "So what happened?"

"I tried to look after my parents," said Marjie. "And of course, they'd accept food and tea from me, but their sadness was so overwhelming. They never really recovered. They're gone now, of course. Graham, well, a year later, after an argument with my father, declared that he would not take over the family business as he was expected to. Instead, he took off for the city. My father's shop was already struggling because he didn't have the energy for it anymore. Graham washed his hands of it, and of all of us."

"That sounds like an incredibly stressful time for the family," said Delia.

"Indeed," Marjie agreed. "Graham decided he didn't want to stay in Myrtlewood anymore. He said he was rejecting the entire magical world because it was to blame for Jowell's death. He responded to the whole situation by shutting us all out. We haven't spoken for decades. Even when my parents died, Graham held the bare minimum of services for them and wouldn't exchange words with me at all. Perhaps he blamed me too. Perhaps he thought that because I was better at magic, I should have protected my brother. I always felt terribly guilty about that."

"That's hardly your fault," said Delia. "It's a tragic thing that happened, but it's normal for people to look for somebody else to blame in that kind of situation, I'm sure. I suppose Graham inherited the family grimoire?"

She nodded sadly. "Along with everything else, not that there was much to inherit. We were always a fairly modest family and the shop struggled more and more to turn a profit over the years. Graham's an accountant in Yorkshire. It's so far to travel. I suppose I'll have to go there at some point if I need to get my hands on that grimoire. I just don't know if I can face him. The only words he has said to me since Jowell's death have been cold or angry. I suspect he's never processed any of it. I don't think he ever will. I asked about the grimoire once. I wouldn't be surprised if he burned the thing based on the response he gave me. But I can only hope it survived somehow. Maybe he's got it in storage, and I could just sneak in." Marjie paused and then shook her head. "No, I suppose I should at least make an effort to confront him."

Delia patted her friend on the shoulder. "Well, I'm up for a trip to Yorkshire sometime if you like." She smiled.

"That's really sweet of you, dear," said Marjie. "Obviously, we won't have time to go before the solstice, and then there'll be Christmas, but perhaps sometime in the new year."

"We won't need the grimoires before then?" said Delia, feeling like time was quickly running out to figure out her own mystery.

"I don't think so," said Marjie. "From what Agatha has told

me, it sounds like the passage that refers to them is talking about a later stage in unlocking the crone magic. At least we can occupy ourselves with some other things for the time being."

"I suppose so," said Delia. "Why are there so many stages in this magic unlocking business?"

"It seems someone wanted to keep these powers well-hidden," Marjie mused.

Delia sighed. "Well, it's just as well there're more to unlock first, because I have no idea how to get my hands on *my* family grimoire."

"Oh! Look at me, talking all about myself." Marjie chuckled. "I haven't even asked about your situation."

Delia smiled. "That's fine. I haven't known you for long, Marjie, but I'm guessing you're always the one who looks after everyone else, and I'm happy to be here for you. You've gone through a lot recently, by the sounds of it."

Marjie sniffed a little and then focused on her tea. "It's not a bad brew," she said with a kind smile. "I'll have to come over for tea again sometime. Now, tell me, what have you figured out about your family?"

Delia sighed. "Well, as you know, I didn't know anything at all about magic before coming to Myrtlewood. I didn't know I had family around here. However, I did go to the archives. That very odd mayor chatted with me and found me an appropriate book. I gather he has trouble keeping staff."

Marjie chuckled a little. "Can you imagine working closely with Ferg?"

"Heaven forbid," said Delia. "But he was very helpful, I have to say. Apparently, there's quite a history of my family in Myrtlewood, going back many generations. I kind of gathered that based on somehow being one of these elemental crones, but to see it all laid out there..."

"How marvellous," said Marjie. "A whole family history."

"I took a photo," said Delia, pulling up the image on her phone. She handed it to Marjie and then watched as her friend's warm complexion went deathly pale.

"Oh, dear me, not the Bracewells!" said Marjie.

Delia winced. "I heard they might be trouble. Is it that bad?"

"I'm sure whatever you're thinking, it's ten times worse, at least," said Marjie. "You know Rosemary's cousins are Bracewells because her aunt married into the family."

"I take it Rosemary hasn't had the best experience with them," said Delia.

"She's had a lot of trouble, and she's not the only one."

"Tell me more," said Delia. "The more I know, the better at this point."

"Well," said Marjie, "you know how I just told you that my mother came over here as a servant?"

Delia nodded.

"She was originally from Bermuda," said Marjie. "However, as a young lass, she was employed by the Bracewells. They were in Bermuda doing some sort of diplomatic role or something for the witching parliament, I imagine."

This was the first Delia had heard about a witching parliament in Bermuda, but now hardly seemed like the time to ask for details.

"My mother didn't know about all the politics, really," said Marjie. "She just worked in their house. And when they moved to this part of the world, they dragged her along with them, despite the fact that my mother actually wanted to stay with her family. She had no choice, apparently. The Bracewells threatened her and her entire family. Dear old Mum always said they were heartless."

"They sound abhorrent," said Delia.

Marjie nodded. "They were cruel and controlling. Eventually, Mum ran away and married my father, if only to get away from them. Don't get me wrong, my parents had a happy marriage up until they lost their child. But I couldn't help but wonder what my mother would have been like if she hadn't had such a horrible experience early in life."

Delia shuddered. "I'm getting the impression that the family is still rich and haughty, and awful."

"That's also my impression," said Marjie.

"And somehow," said Delia, "I need to get hold of one of their most prized family possessions."

"That appears to be quite a conundrum," said Marjie. "We might need some more tea."

CHAPTER 20

AGATHA

"Oh, for Morrigan's sake!"

Agatha Twigg sat in her favourite high-backed armchair, its soft gold velvet shimmering in the firelight. This was her favourite place to be, surrounded by rows and rows of books in her personal library. It always soothed her, except tonight she grappled with a new level of irritation.

She glanced around for reassurance. The shelves ran from floor to ceiling, each filled with ancient tomes, scrolls, and oddities that only a seasoned witch could appreciate. Her library was a cocoon of knowledge. The flickering firelight from the hearth danced on the spines of the books, casting an ambience of warm, comfortable seclusion.

Beside her on a side table, a decanter and a glass of sherry sat, the glass automatically refilling itself whenever it was low. Which was often. Marla's students might call that 'a life hack for the modern witch', but Agatha merely called it practical. Sherry, like her other favourite beverages, could not be replicated like Marjie's cakes. It took years to brew a fine drop, but it could certainly be served, perpetually, by magic.

Yet still, despite all this, discomfort nagged at her mind.

She huffed impatiently, flipping through her ancient family grimoire. She had been searching through it for hours, her mind racing with Ingrid's recent revelations. The grimoire was old, a relic filled with spells and lore that spanned generations.

"Ingrid, you cryptic crossword of a woman, what were you hinting at?" Agatha mumbled, annoyed and intrigued in equal measure.

Agatha took another sip of her sherry, grateful for the charm she'd placed on it years ago that ensured she'd never feel anything but delight from her indulgences. It was important to enjoy life's small pleasures. After all, if you couldn't cheat a little, what was the point of being a witch?

Her favourite libations didn't addle her health, she never felt the dreadful effects of drunkenness or hangovers, and she was absolutely convinced that alcoholism was no risk to her, no matter what Marjie thought about the subject.

Her eyes were beginning to tire as they scanned the worn pages of her family grimoire, each leaf filled with recipes for potions, incantations, and magical histories. The book was an heirloom, passed down through countless generations, each witch adding her own chapter, her own discoveries. She was searching for something – anything – that could explain what

Ingrid had hinted at earlier. Her own book was apparently connected to the newly-discovered crone grimoire, and the thought had left her intrigued and, admittedly, slightly vexed.

She grumbled as page after ancient page offered her only silly old trifles: spells for better butter, incantations for less creaky knees, and a particularly nasty hex aimed at noisy neighbours. The book seemed to be mocking her, and more than anything, Agatha prided herself on having good relationships with books. She gave it a stern talking to.

Ingrid's words gnawed at her. Was her grimoire really connected to that dreadfully important book they'd recently salvaged?

The brittle pages passed under her fingertips – recipes for invisibility potions, half-baked incantations for love spells, and infuriating marginalia about why Uncle Henry was never to be trusted with canapés.

"Ridiculous!"

She closed the book, then opened it again at the beginning.

As her finger traced lines of ink that had been laid down before the invention of the printing press, something changed.

Taking another sip of her sherry, savouring the complex flavours that danced on her tongue, she flipped another page. That's when she felt it – a subtle shift in the texture beneath her finger. Her eyes narrowed. Pulling her spectacles down to the tip of her nose, she peered closely at the page.

A faint jolt of magic sparked at her fingertip.

She stared down at the book, her mouth opening in surprise

as words appeared on the page, right beneath her finger, and scrawled themselves across the parchment.

Words in unfamiliar handwriting.

No, that wasn't quite right. It was, in fact, handwriting she had only recently become acquainted with: the same script as that in the Crone grimoire.

At first, the words made no sense and she grumbled to herself about the older style of language not limited by the standard spellings which came after the invention of the dictionary.

Drawing a shuddering breath, Agatha read aloud:

Gret bestes shall wyke with eld'r crone majiks, ye anc't maygiks awake, ye drakons sall rise

The room seemed to darken, as if the very walls absorbed the gravity of the words. Agatha leaned back, her heart pounding. The walls seemed to close in around her. The sherry, which had been a source of comfort, now sat untouched, its charm suddenly inconsequential. The mysteries unfolding before her were larger than any charm, and for the first time in many years, Agatha Twigg felt the gravity of the path they had all started to walk.

The line spoke of great beasts awakening in tandem with their crone powers. This sounded more like a warning than some line from a spell as Ingrid had suggested. What trouble had the old bat got them into this time?

A chill coursed down her spine, settling deep in her bones despite the heat from the roaring fire.

"What in Cerridwen's cauldron are we meddling with?" she muttered.

Agatha leaned back in her chair, her eyes staring blankly at the book but seeing far beyond it. Her mind raced, piecing together ancient myths and arcane theories. She had felt invincible with their recent magical discoveries, empowered and untouchable. She'd even felt a subtle shift in her own powers, over the past few days. She had not quite put her finger on exactly what had changed, but she'd experienced a lightness, a clarity of mind, which was now swiftly counteracted by heavy thoughts of doom.

Even the sherry in her glass seemed to pause, as if holding its liquid breath. The cogs and wheels of ancient fate were turning, and the hands on destiny's clock pointed toward uncertainty.

The words in her grimoire had served as a sobering reminder: magic, especially of the ancient sort, was not to be trifled with.

She shuddered as the words echoed in her head, heavy with foreboding. It was as though the room itself had darkened, despite the warm glow from the hearth. What were they getting themselves into? What ancient forces were stirring alongside their newfound powers?

Agatha Twigg felt the full force of her age bear down on her – and the weight of something far older. The grimoire closed with a puff of ancient dust, as if agreeing with her.

"More sherry, I think," she said to no one in particular. The decanter, naturally, complied. After all, what was the use of magic if not to make life a smidgen more bearable, especially when that life was about to get alarmingly interesting?

Agatha sighed. Of course, the Order had spoken of dragons and great beasts before, but it was mere hearsay until she'd read it in a reliable book. It was all well and good to unlock the powers of yesteryears; it was another thing entirely to unleash old nightmares alongside them. She took another sip, allowing the sherry to fortify her courage. If dragons were stirring, she would need more than wit and spells. But for now, those would have to do.

She felt her resolve harden. They had embarked on this path of discovery, stepping onto a winding road filled with both peril and promise. They had awakened something that had lain dormant, probably for centuries, and now they had no choice but to see it through, come what may. With a newfound sense of purpose and a sliver of dread, Agatha Twigg closed her grimoire, took another sip of her sherry, and steeled herself for the challenges that lay ahead.

CHAPTER 21
DELIA

Anticipation shimmered through her. The crowd hushed. The lights dimmed.

"Break a leg, Delia," the stage manager whispered from the wings, a phrase that suddenly felt ominous.

The curtains rose, the red velvet clearing the way, and Delia stepped out onto the stage.

This was the moment she'd been waiting for: her starring role, the debut of the show she'd been working so hard to bring to life. She took a deep breath, turning up towards the crowd. The spotlight caught her eyelashes, so that she could only dimly see the hundreds of faces staring at her. She took one final step, reaching for the lines that she'd recited a hundred times in rehearsal. Just at that moment, there was a cracking sound; her heel gave way and her body collapsed onto the floor.

She screamed, everything slipping away from her as she fell through the darkness.

Delia woke, sweating and crying out, relieved to find that she was no longer a young woman experiencing the most embarrassing moment of her career – and probably her life.

It had been so many years ago. She rarely thought of it these days, but that moment changed her life. Perhaps the change was for the best. After all, the incident was the reason she'd stopped acting, and eventually returned to the theatre as a director instead.

At the time though, the pain, the shame, the embarrassment had borne down on her.

There had been months where she couldn't face herself, let alone the public.

The terrible reviews, the profound disappointment, the scorn she'd faced – she'd somehow managed to tuck all of that away.

Out of sight. Out of mind.

And yet, it was a vivid memory. The dream was haunting.

She took a deep breath, calming herself, thankful that now, in her sixties, she didn't give a damn.

Life had gone on; she'd had a brilliant career. Even if she never returned to it now, she'd done a fabulous job and she had more important things to think about, such as keeping her daughter and grandchildren safe, and understanding this brilliant yet terrifying magical world.

The past is the past, she assured herself. *Everything got much better after that terrible night...eventually.*

She suppressed the dread that everything might now be indeed about to get much worse.

After what felt like hours, but was probably only twenty minutes or so, she calmed herself enough to fall back asleep. But it was a fitful sleep; more disturbing dreams awaited her.

She was in the theatre again; this time a young woman with white hair was pointing at her, laughing. The sound was shrill, grating on her nerves.

"You'll never escape your past, Delia!" the woman cackled.

She was chased by circus performers, their painted faces twisted into grotesque smiles, and then finally, a great fiery dragon, its scales shimmering in the dream-light, roared and lunged at her. Delia ran for her life, her feet pounding on the imaginary ground.

She awoke, blessedly safe in her bed, but anxious. Dawn's light crept through the drawn curtains and more sleep was pointless now, especially when it might lead to further nightmares. Instead, she lay there, stretching out the usual tensions in her neck and back, and pondering what it all might mean.

The visions she'd had at Ingrid's house had supposedly

meant something, and her dreams of late certainly seemed to mean something, though all of that was still so unclear.

Delia was only beginning to untangle her grandmother's legacy, but it seemed important now. Her dreams were frustratingly unclear, leaving her more confused than ever. The only thing she could do was brush them aside, yet again, and set her day back on-course with a strong coffee or two.

CHAPTER 22
THE CLERIC

The Cleric paced the length of his office, the rug underfoot barely muffling the sound of his footfalls. The walls, adorned with ancient texts and maps marked with esoteric symbols, seemed to close in on him. Normally, they offered comfort, a reminder of tradition and purpose, but today they felt like witnesses to his moral quandary. Even the ambient warmth from the hearth seemed to taunt him, contrasting starkly with the icy dread that filled his veins.

His fingers brushed across the edge of his desk, stopping at a parchment that lay there. He looked at it as though it were a viper ready to strike. Father Benedict had always said, "The less you know, the better". It was a guiding principle in an order shrouded in secrets and mysteries. A principle that the Cleric had followed without question – until now.

He picked up the parchment from his desk again, his hands

almost trembling. The ink seemed to mock him, the words a snare set by some malevolent force. Father Benedict might think keeping everyone in the dark was for the best, but these instructions left the Cleric flummoxed and appalled. It was a directive that scraped against every fibre in his being, something so horrendous it could corrupt his soul beyond redemption.

Surely the elders couldn't have approved this. Surely the Almighty would cast severe judgement upon everyone involved in such a plan.

The air tasted stale, despite the room's usually comforting scent of burning wood and old tomes. He drew in a shaky breath, each inhalation a battle between his duty and his conscience. How could this be what the Order demanded of him?

His eyes darted to the fireplace. Normally, its flames danced with inviting warmth, a centrepiece in a room filled with ancient knowledge and mystical artefacts. Now, however, it seemed more a purveyor of shadow than light, casting odd shapes that flickered menacingly against the surrounding walls. He wondered, not for the first time, whether his soul would cast similar dark shades if he proceeded as instructed.

His tongue felt dry; he moved to a cabinet and poured himself a glass of water from a crystal decanter, but even the cool liquid did nothing to cleanse the distaste that rose within him.

He took another deep, shuddering breath and lowered himself into his chair. It creaked beneath him, a haunting note that sounded like a warning. His finger hovered above the parchment as if it were a piece of hot coal. He wanted to throw it into the fire, to watch the ink blister and the paper curl into ash. To pretend he had never received these instructions, that this was nothing but a figment of a very bad dream.

But he couldn't. His hands, almost of their own accord, folded the parchment and set it back down on his desk. He felt nauseous, his stomach a whirlpool of dread and guilt. Father Benedict's words rang in his ears, a mantra that no longer offered solace but instead felt like chains binding him to a destiny he never asked for.

He was the Cleric of the Order of Crimson, a man who had vowed to serve, to obey. But as he sat back down, staring into the dancing flames that seemed almost whimsical in their movement, he found himself questioning his vows.

The plan was horrendous, beyond any act he'd ever thought he'd be a part of. This was not just bending morality; this was shattering it.

What kind of trouble was he getting himself into? What shadow would be cast on his soul if he followed through with this operation?

Sure, the Order had done many questionable things in pursuit of the higher good, but none involved such potential brutality or risked the purity of the souls involved in quite this way.

"I am my honour and my duty," he whispered to himself, the words a shallow affirmation of his chosen path. But as he spoke, he couldn't help but feel that something within him had irrevocably shifted. He was still the Cleric, yes, but one who had glimpsed the price of blind obedience, and it was a price that weighed heavily on his soul.

He paused and looked at the document one last time, his eyes catching the detail he had consciously avoided acknowledging, as though saying it would make it all too real.

He shuddered.

The plans involved: *a woman*.

CHAPTER 23
DELIA

Delia took her last sip of coffee and looked out towards the back garden, wondering if she should give her powers another try.

"No, that's enough for one morning," she assured herself.

She cast her eyes across the room to a stack of boxes. Kitty had been tremendously efficient, as always. She'd managed to get Delia's bond back and had a moving company pack up her tiny apartment and deliver her things to the house, all without setting foot in that dreadful little place again. Delia was yet to unpack, aside from her wardrobe, mostly because she was still enjoying avoiding thinking about the dreadful interlude, after Jerry announced their impending divorce, where she spend a lot of time moping around the apartment feeling sorry for herself, which had never really been her style.

Delia put her cup down and frowned.

With only two more days until the solstice, the Crones had been busy. Well, Agatha, Marjie, and Ingrid all seemed to be incredibly busy. Delia, not knowing exactly how she could be of use, had found herself at rather a loose end. She couldn't help Marjie prepare spells and charms, which might be lobbed explosively at the Order of Crimson as they disrupted the winter solstice ritual. She was not much use helping with research, and Agatha preferred to research alone anyway. Delia didn't know where to start with the big old musty books of scrawled handwriting in a range of different languages. And Ingrid's preparations seemed to involve a lot of scrying, something that Delia only found incredibly confusing. Most recently, Ingrid had taken to sipping herbal tea concoctions while staring out at the woods around her house, 'listening to the forest'. All Delia could hear was birdsong and the rustling of leaves, not adding terribly a lot of information.

She wondered, not for the first time, whether there had been some kind of mistake. Surely, if she had some family who'd been involved in magic for years there would be a more suitable Crone to take up the mantle among them.

She glanced at the image of her family tree again, but having no real context for any of the names, it didn't really do her much good.

The consolation prize for not being useful was, of course, that Delia had plenty of spare time. A blessing and a curse.

She did quite enjoy herself, because that was her policy: to make the most of life in whatever way she could.

Time seemed to be moving agonisingly slowly, as if the icy weather had reduced it to a glacial pace.

Delia had only been in Myrtlewood for a couple of weeks, after all, and in that time, she'd managed to go on a ridiculous goat-cart quest and retrieve an important magical artefact whilst being relentlessly hunted by red-cloaked buffoons, made three new friends – only one of whom made her entirely comfortable – and moved to a new house. Some of this change had been as seamless as if fate was rowing her along in a little boat; other things had been rather difficult to adjust to, including her own magic, which was *still* not behaving itself.

Every morning, as early as possible, Delia had continued to practice, to no avail. It was as if the trying itself was getting in the way of achieving any results, which was probably the case. She didn't know how to try without trying. That was infuriating, and infuriating scenarios only seemed to make her light rather dangerous fires on any surface that happened to be around her at the time, regardless of how flammable it was supposed to be.

She was certainly not at the stage where she could claim any kind of mastery, but she reminded herself this whole situation was incredibly new to her.

The magical world certainly had its perks. The creams from the apothecary had done an amazing job, making her feel fresh and youthful, bringing back a glowing complexion she had missed in recent years. The local spa would surely have even more treats in store but unfortunately it was closed for the holiday period into the new year, so instead, Delia decided to go back to the apothecary and see what else they might have.

She dressed warmly to suit the crisp morning air and left her little house with the unnerving feeling that she was being watched.

She enjoyed the brief stroll into the village, admiring its wintery glory.

Delia walked into the quaint little town, adorned now with an enormous icy dome covering its centre, sparkling in the sunlight in eager anticipation of the winter solstice which Delia was dreading.

She pushed her worries away and stopped to collect a small package of her favourite rose and cayenne truffles from Papa Jack at Myrtlewood Chocolates, and then proceeded on to the apothecary.

The woman she'd met briefly last time, with the long blonde hair – Ashwyn – was standing behind the counter and smiled as she entered.

"Nice to see you again," said Ashwyn. "How can I help?"

"You know, I bought some face cream from you the other day, and it was marvellous," Delia said. "I was wondering what other kinds of goodies you might have."

"Would you like a consultation?" Ashwyn asked, brushing her long wavy hair back over her shoulder with willowy grace.

"A consultation?" Delia raised an eyebrow.

"I'm a qualified medical herbalist," Ashwyn explained. "When I consult with clients I ask them a few questions and then mix them up a special formula of tinctures and charms to help with whatever ails them."

Delia smiled. "That sounds magical."

"It often is," Ashwyn assured her.

She handed Delia a cup of peppermint and valerian tea and then led her through to the back of the shop.

Unlike many back rooms of stores, it wasn't cramped and cluttered. It was a nice, clear space, elegantly arranged with herbs and flowers in vases strategically placed around the room.

"So tell me about yourself," Ashwyn asked Delia as they settled into comfortable armchairs. Ashwyn posed a lot of questions ranging from normal ones about past health experiences and diet, sleep, and pain, to the more unusual questions such as, "Are there any particular crystals you're drawn to?" or "What's your favourite direction?" and "What's your first thought upon waking in the morning?"

"Don't suppose there's a tonic for both achy joints and bad dreams, is there?" Delia asked. "Because if there is, that's the one I need."

Ashwyn smiled warmly at her. "I'll see what I can do. You can go and browse in the shop if you like, or stay here if you prefer. I'll just be a few minutes mixing something up for you."

Delia returned to the apothecary shop so that she could try out more of the skin creams. A sense of heaviness was plaguing her, and she wondered whether that was something she should tell Ashwyn about.

As Delia applied a tiny dab of eye cream that promised to

lighten dark circles she had a creeping sensation across her spine.

She turned back towards the window of the apothecary and caught a glimpse of a man in a hat, his handsome, weathered face staring right through her.

The Cowboy.

But she blinked, and he was gone again.

Delia shook her head. He couldn't possibly have been there. She must be seeing things.

Was he watching her somehow? That strange and compelling man who'd followed her to Myrtlewood, who'd ridden with her enemies and yet had stared right through her while the invisibility spell had protected her and the other Crones from the Order of Crimson – none of whom were able to see or hear the four women as they left that abandoned town.

The Cowboy could see them, and yet he didn't alert anyone to their presence; he merely winked.

The memory sent a shiver of discomfort through Delia as she stood there in the shop. Perhaps he had a more devious plan; perhaps he was stalking her even now. The creeping sensation intensified, and a small flame erupted from the light. Delia gasped and flung out her arms, which only exacerbated the flames.

Ashwyn rushed out with a bucket of water, dousing the fire.

"I'm so sorry," Delia said, fanning away the smoke with her hands. "I thought I had that under control."

Ashwyn dismissed her with a wave as if spontaneous combustion was all in a day's work.

"I don't suppose you could pop anything in my potion to stop me setting things on fire at random?" Delia asked.

"Perhaps something a little more calming would help," Ashwyn suggested, smiling serenely.

Delia struggled to regain her composure. "I'm afraid I'm rather a liability."

Ashwyn's smile only broadened. "It certainly keeps life interesting."

CHAPTER 24
ELAMINA

E lamina frowned at Cornwall winter air, the scent of salt ice. Her car pulled up to the imposing façade of the Bracewell-Thorn mansion, a grand structure that loomed out of the fog like a ghostly apparition. Only hours ago she'd been in Bermuda, ensconced in the warm, tropical air and attending to diplomatic matters at the witching parliament, when the message came through from Aunt Sabrina.

"Return home at once," her great aunt had commanded. "It's a family emergency."

Stepping out of the car, the chill air seeped through her clothes, a stark contrast to the balmy climate she'd left behind.

She walked into the mansion, her heels clicking on the marble floor, echoing through the cavernous hall.

Her aunt greeted her coolly, her eyes scanning Elamina's outfit from head to toe.

"Ah, so that's what young people are wearing these days," she said, her voice dripping with disdain.

Elamina hardly felt young, but compared to Aunt Sabrina – with her hair impeccably coiffed in a style befitting Queen Victoria, and her wrinkles betraying years of stern expressions – she was practically a child.

"Fashion evolves, Aunt," Elamina replied primly, maintaining her composure.

Aunt Sabrina held her gaze for a moment as if waiting for some further reaction, always on the lookout for any sign of weakness she could stamp out. It was a family trait she had in common with Elamina's parents.

"Would you care for some artemisia tea?" her aunt offered finally, leading her into the drawing room.

"That would be fine, thank you."

Elamina relaxed slightly as she entered the room filled with the scent of old books and the musty aroma of antique furniture.

Clearly, this emergency wasn't so urgent as to get in the way of tea.

Elamina took a seat on one of the antique chairs, its fabric worn but still emanating an air of grandeur. She should really have these re-covered when her aunt returned to London and hope the old woman didn't notice when she returned. Family homes were always a nightmare to maintain. The balance between tradition and opulence had to be carefully navigated and everyone seemed to have an opinion on updates that might threaten the old ways, even when it came to upholstery.

A servant entered with a tray, setting down a cup of steaming tea in front of Elamina. The herbal aroma filled the air, mingling with the room's existing scents.

"So, what's this emergency that required me to leave my work?" Elamina asked, getting straight to the point.

Aunt Sabrina's eyes narrowed, her lips tightening. She took a shaky breath. "Someone has accessed the family records in Myrtlewood!" she said, her voice cracking with outrage in a rare showing of emotion.

Elamina felt a surge of indignation rise within her. She'd been pulled away from important diplomatic work for *this*? But she suppressed her reaction, as she'd been trained to do since childhood.

Bracewells do not make a scene, after all.

"The records were accessed?" Elamina asked, her voice perfectly even.

Her aunt glared at her. "I had special charms laid so that no one could access those records, other than family. Yet, they've been tampered with," her aunt continued, her voice returning to its usual icy tones though her hands trembled slightly in her lap.

Elamina raised an eyebrow, her interest piqued. Perhaps there was something more devious afoot than some filing clerk poking their nose into a dusty old book. "Who would dare to access these records, and for what purpose?"

"That's what I expect you to attend to," Aunt Sabrina said, her voice quivering with barely contained anger, "and make sure they regret it."

Elamina took a sip of her artemisia tea, savouring the soothing aromatic bitterness and warmth that spread through her body, yet maintaining her icy exterior.

"I will see to it," she assured her aunt.

A quick trip to the mayor's office in Myrtlewood was all it took to extract the relevant information. After asking the right questions of the rather odd new mayor, she had everything she needed.

To Elamina's surprise, it wasn't a stranger who had accessed the records; it was a distant cousin, newly arrived in Myrtlewood. Her curiosity was more than a small flame, it was a raging inferno.

Moments later she arrived in front of a modest row of terraced houses.

This was hardly the sort of property anyone in her family would deign to inherit – except perhaps her ridiculous Thorn cousin, who would probably call it "charming".

Elamina brushed away her hesitation like an inconvenient spiderweb and walked confidently up the path.

She knocked at the door, and moments later it was opened by woman, likely in her fifties or sixties. The woman was well-groomed, except for her wild hair streaked with an incorrigible shade of red. The scent of lavender and something spicy – perhaps cinnamon – wafted from inside the house.

Elamina looked the woman dead in the eye. "You must be Delia," she said, her voice as cool as ice.

This woman might be a relative, but she certainly was not a

Bracewell. And Elamina was determined to find out just what she was up to and put a stop to it.

CHAPTER 25
DELIA

Delia squinted across the table at the woman who'd appeared on her doorstep moments before. She looked familiar somehow.

This so-called cousin, Elamina, did not smile, and so Delia resisted the people-pleasing urge to grin at her.

Elamina sipped the coffee Delia had made her as if it might be the worst and most dangerous thing she'd ever consumed, as though she was trying to prove that she was tough enough to handle it.

Her clothing looked terribly expensive, matching her haughty demeanour.

Delia was not one to be impressed by hoity-toity people; in fact, in her experience, they tended to be rather boring.

This Elamina, however, was somewhat of a puzzle. Not

entirely boring, but Delia couldn't quite put a finger on what was interesting about her.

Then, as Elamina put her cup down and glanced across, her eyes flashed with a familiar fire. Delia realised there was something familiar about this cousin, and it wasn't just a family resemblance.

"You were in my dream," Delia said flatly, as though demanding some kind of explanation from the woman she'd never met before in person.

Elamina raised an eyebrow. "I was?" she said blandly, as if this was quite a normal thing.

Delia felt a slight surge of rage, recalling how the Elamina in her dream had pointed and laughed at her on stage, like her audience had done when she'd fallen.

However, Elamina couldn't possibly have been there that night at the theatre all those years ago, could she? And it seemed ridiculous to assume that she'd played a conscious role in a dream.

Delia shook her head. "So, we're related and you've tracked me down because?"

"Like I said," Elamina replied with a small frown. "My aunt was concerned that somebody was looking at the family records. She called me back from Bermuda, where I have quite important work to do, you know."

"Oh, do you?" said Delia politely, as if entertaining the whims and fancies of a small child.

Elamina glared at her. "Yes," she replied. "I take it you're new to magic?" She said this as if it was some kind of incredibly distasteful thing.

"I can't help that," said Delia defensively. "I've heard it happens sometimes. In fact, I've heard you have another cousin who came to magic rather late in life. Rosemary Thorn." She said this deliberately, because Delia suspected she might get a rise out of Elamina, given what Marjie had said about the animosity between the two.

"Rosemary is lovely, isn't she?" Delia continued, watching Elamina's mouth twist in distaste.

"There's no accounting for taste," Elamina retorted.

"Have you tracked me down merely to insult me?" said Delia calmly. "Or is there some other reason?"

Of course, Delia had a reason to engage in communications with her long lost Bracewell family, but she wasn't about to lay all her cards out on the table. At least not yet.

Elamina coughed and then took another sip of coffee and grimaced. She regained her composure and looked Delia dead in the eye.

"You're powerful," she said, as though this was some kind of problem that ought to be discussed.

"Yes," said Delia flatly, not giving an inch.

Elamina stared at her for a moment, and her mouth quirked as though she might, under all of that haughtiness, rather prefer to smile.

This only made Delia laugh, and Elamina watched her, eyes bulging in horror.

"Yes, I am powerful," said Delia. "What of it?"

Elamina took a deep breath. "The power that you have is a family power."

"Oh, is it?" said Delia. "Well, I suppose it'd be in our best interests then if I learned all about the family, considering that I'm part of it."

Elamina's eyes narrowed and she folded her arms. "I don't know what you've heard about the Bracewell-Thorns, or the Bracewells in general," she said, "but I must admit we are not the most open or forthcoming lineage. However, you do appear to belong to us."

She said that last part as though Delia were a pet cat dragging in a dead rat.

"Oh, do I now?" said Delia.

Elamina shrugged. "Albeit through a stray, straggling line…"

"I figured as much," said Delia. She pulled up the photo of the family tree on her phone, looking at the names.

Elamina wrinkled her nose. "You took a picture of our family tree on your telephone?"

Delia laughed again. "I know you're not trying to be amusing, love, but I'm afraid I can't help myself."

Elamina looked away. "At least one of us is having a good time," she muttered.

"Look," Delia said, leaning forward. "Let's get down to business."

"I knew it!" Elamina's eyes sparked with suspicion. "Is it money you want?"

"Of course not," said Delia. "What kind of person tracks down their long-lost family just to ask for money? I'm quite alright here. This isn't my house...well, my situation is complicated, and I'm not going to go into it."

"I'm aware of your situation," said Elamina. "You're in the process of divorce, you have one child and two grandchildren, and you're quite a prominent director in the theatre."

She said that as though it was some kind of criminal record, which only made Delia laugh more.

"I see you've done your research," Delia said.

"I'm thorough," said Elamina. "But I don't know what it is you want, Delia."

Delia let out a slow sigh. "Look, if it was up to me, I would want nothing at all from you. Although I must admit, I'm curious to know a little more about the family. I wasn't particularly close to my parents, you see. My grandmother, she was marvellous, but she died when I was young. Now I've discovered she's got this magical lineage, and this whole family."

"You want to *know* us?" said Elamina, as if this was an outrageous thing to suggest.

"I'm not a hundred percent sure about that," Delia admitted. "I can't say you have a particularly positive reputation. Not necessarily you, in particular," she clarified. After all, she didn't want to make another enemy just yet, not when there were already plenty of powerful forces after her.

"There's something else, isn't there?" said Elamina. "Are you going to tell me what it is?"

This was the time to show her cards, perhaps, but Delia hesitated. If Elamina and the rest of the Bracewells knew what she wanted, perhaps that would put her at a disadvantage.

"There are some things that I'd like to know about the family, and the history of our magic," Delia said.

"For what purpose?" Elamina asked, her posture stiffening.

"Well, wouldn't you, in my position?" said Delia reasonably. "I just discovered that I'm a witch. I have this power which causes me to cast small infernos everywhere I go if I'm not careful. I've set more things on fire by accident than I care to admit in the last week or two. And a lot of strange things have happened."

She hesitated, not wanting to tell Elamina about her dealings with the Order of Crimson; who knew what kinds of dangerous secret societies the dastardly Bracewells might be involved in, after all?

"I have a lot of questions," Delia said.

"Such as?" Elamina asked.

"How do I control my power?" said Delia.

Elamina gave her a pitying look. "I'm not in the business of aiding newly awakened witches. I wouldn't begin to know how to train someone who wasn't already a master." She brushed back a strand of her silver blonde hair.

"Fair enough," said Delia. "Were you born knowing how to use your powers, then?"

"It's hard to recall," said Elamina nonchalantly. "I've always been gifted, on both sides of my family."

"Oh yes, you're related to the Thorns," said Delia, with a warm amusement in her tone. "I hear Rosemary is incredibly powerful."

Delia smiled benignly.

Elamina's eyes flashed with rage. "You're trying to taunt me, aren't you?"

"Only because you make it too easy," Delia replied.

Elamina's shoulders slumped slightly. "I don't want to like you," she admitted, "but I sort of do."

"I have a fabulous personality," Delia offered in a consoling tone. "It's hard not to like me, I'm afraid."

"I wish I could say the same for myself," said Elamina.

"For someone with fiery magic, you are a little cold in how you come across," Delia said. "But you don't have to be, you know."

"I like myself the way I am," said Elamina.

"And that's why," said Delia, "as much as I don't want to like someone who's snobby and haughty and rude to me, I must admit that I do quite like you, cousin."

A small but genuine smile spread across Elamina's face before it faded back into its icy, practiced expression. "There are lots of things you're not telling me," she said evenly.

"I've only just met you," said Delia. "And I'm sure there are plenty of things you're not telling me, but perhaps we can meet again."

"Perhaps," Elamina replied, as she lifted her hand in farewell.

CHAPTER 26
INGRID

Ingrid settled onto the timeworn steps of her hut, feeling the grooves and knots of the wood press into her thighs like an old, unreadable map. The air was cool and sweet, filling her lungs with the perfumed blend of pine, damp earth, and the faintest trace of wildflowers. Her fingers grazed the rough surface of the wooden railing, every splinter and imperfection a sentence in a story only she could read.

There was only so much planning and plotting that could be done to prepare for the solstice, and Marjie and Agatha seemed to have that side of things under control. They were at their respective homes, bustling with activity. Agatha was studiously researching while Marjie was brewing up all kinds of charms, from those suitable for attacking enemies to some more befitting of hosting afternoon tea. Meanwhile, Delia was trying to get her own powers under control, which was about the most useful thing she could do given her circumstances and newness to magic.

Ingrid refused to be busy. It wasn't her style.

Being busy was often a mere excuse, a convenient way to avoid reality. It rather got in the way of more useful things, such as listening.

Her eyes closed gently, the yellowish light filtering through her eyelids transforming the world into a peaceful haze. She inhaled deeply, drawing the scent of the forest into her nostrils, a comforting blend of resinous sap, decaying leaves, and the indefinable freshness of living plants. She tuned her ears to the choral backdrop of nature – birdsongs as intricate as any sonnet, rustling leaves like a soft, persistent drumroll, and the distant murmur of flowing water, a tranquil bass line underpinning it all.

Slowly, the boundaries between her and the forest blurred. It felt as if her own heartbeat and the pulse of the forest had melded into one – each beat drawing her deeper into a trance. She was no longer a solitary entity but a note in a grand orchestral score, each element of nature contributing to a harmonious masterpiece of coexistence.

Her senses expanded, and she perceived more than just the physical world. She felt the thriving life force of each tree, the resonance of the lichen and moss, the quicksilver thoughts of woodland creatures, the subtle pulse of mycelium through the earth, and the slow, wise consciousness of the ancient stones. The forest seemed to breathe with her, every inhalation drawing her deeper into awareness of the patterns of life, every exhalation releasing a puff of her own worries and fears into the ever-accepting embrace of nature.

The stunning beauty of the forest unfolded around her. A spider in its web was as important as the towering oak, each playing a part in a miraculous shared existence. The forest's grandeur was not just a large stand of trees but a living, sentient presence.

As she listened, something intruded upon the harmony – a dark shadow that made the hairs on the back of her neck stand up. The forest's rhythm faulted, like a missed beat. A dissonant note sent a ripple through the entire woodland.

An ominous sense suddenly gripped her – a feeling as if the earth beneath her and the air around her had both thickened and thinned simultaneously. The forest's pulse quickened, matching her own rising heartbeat.

And then it came, a shiver of foreboding that swept through the interwoven strands of life around her, seeping into the very core of her being. The warning wasn't audible or visible; it was an intuition, an inexplicable knowing.

Her eyes shot open, the serene forest suddenly appearing as a stage upon which something unknown and inescapable was about to unfold. The momentary peace shattered, Ingrid knew one thing for sure: an unnameable, unpredictable change was coming, and it was coming soon.

With a sigh, Ingrid grumbled, "No amount of plotting and planning can prepare you for the unexpected."

CHAPTER 27

MATHILDA

The sun caressed her skin with gentle warmth. The scent of lavender and sage filled the air, mingling with the distant sound of the sisters' chants. Young Mathilda ran her hands through her hair, the locks her mother said were like spun gold. The other children darted between the herb beds, their laughter a melody in the serene garden.

Ingrid was there too, older and bolder, her feet bare against the cool earth. "Catch me if you can!" she called, her voice carrying a freedom that Mathilda envied. Ingrid's presence was like a wildflower amongst the orderly rows of herbs – untamed, vibrant.

The sensation of sage leaves brushing against her hands as she searched for Ingrid was vivid. The herbs whispered secrets, secrets that only Ingrid seemed to understand.

"You can't just always do what other people tell you," Ingrid *teased, emerging from behind a large rose bush, her eyes alight with mischief and defiance.*

Mathilda knew her sister was different. Ingrid spoke to the plants, listened to the wind, and stubbornly questioned everything the Sisterhood taught.

"Why must you always follow the rules?" Ingrid asked, just as she had many times, her gaze fixed on the world beyond the clochar walls.

Mathilda protested, and now Ingrid's words were sharp with passion.

"There's more to life than this!"

Time shifted, and the scene grew darker as years elapsed. They were both grown now. The waning moon was setting in the sky, and Mathilda watched as her sister walked away, leaving their only home.

Mathilda, torn between loyalty and love, pleaded with her to stay, to not venture into the unknown, but Ingrid's mind was set, and she carried on without a backward glance.

"We shall meet again, sister, but you have your life and I have mine. Farewell."

Awakening from the dream, Mathilda lay still for a moment, the echoes of Ingrid's voice and the scent of the herb garden lingering in her senses. It was dawn now, and while the Clochar was quiet, it was a suitable time to make a visit. She rose, a newfound determination in her step, and made her way to Sister Breag's chambers.

The stone corridors of the Veiled Sisterhood's compound

echoed around her along with her footsteps. Mathilda's heart pounded with the weight of the words she needed to say.

She found Sister Breag at her desk, surrounded by ancient tomes, her face illuminated by candlelight. Without preamble, Mathilda spoke. "Sister Breag, we need to discuss Ingrid's return. Is it truly right to force her back?"

Breag looked up, her eyes searching Mathilda's face. "Child, the threads of fate are not ours to question."

Mathilda's resolve hardened. "But Ingrid always believed we create our own destiny. She never accepted that our paths were predetermined."

Breag sighed, her gaze drifting to a candle's flickering flame. "Ingrid's spirit was always untamed, like her mother's. But we must trust in the greater design."

Mathilda felt a pang of sorrow at the mention of their mother. "But if this design harms her, what then? What about her choice, her freedom?"

"Do not fear, Mathilda," Breag reassured her, her voice softening. "All will unfold as it should, but now is not the time. The Oracles tell us we must all be patient. The day will come, eventually, and you will understand. Destiny has its way."

Mathilda left the chamber, her thoughts swirling in a tense storm. She understood the Sisterhood's aims, but Ingrid's fierce independence echoed in her heart. She knew better than to challenge her sister's spirit. As she walked back to her chamber, Mathilda pondered the balance between destiny and choice.

In her heart, she longed to protect her sister, no matter what the future held, and yet Ingrid had always been a troublemaker, bringing all kinds of problems and even delighting in them. Mathilda sighed as she began to prepare for the day.

Perhaps the elder sisters were right. Fate would play out, regardless of her conflicting values. Mathilda might worry for Ingrid, as she always had done, but Ingrid was a wily old bat and could take care of herself.

Her love for her biological sister had always been there, but Ingrid had left her, abandoned her out of nothing more than her own selfish desire for adventure. As Mathilda looked in the mirror, seeing her hair that was now white rather than gold, she had to admit to herself that her own loyalty had always been to the sisterhood.

CHAPTER 28
DELIA

D elia found herself feeling unusually cheerful the following morning, almost as if a warm ray of sunshine was shining right through her. Even her unruly powers hadn't affected her mood. She smiled to herself as she stepped into Marjie's tea shop to pick up some treats for lunch.

"You're looking chipper today," said Marjie, beaming at her.

"Actually, I'm feeling great. I don't even know why. Perhaps it's Ashwyn's amazing tonic. I tried it last night, and I had no horrible, haunting dreams at all. I felt so much better this morning."

"Good to hear," said Marjie. "I might just have to ask her what her secret is."

Delia smiled again and surveyed the cabinet of pastries, deli-cious-looking sandwiches, and scones – all kinds of delicious, starchy treats that Jerry would never have approved of when they were married. He always was such a Puritan, that man.

Delia often wondered these days why she'd put up with him for so long. They'd had their own separate lives in many ways, aside from the theatre business, of course. That had been their shared project, and perhaps it had kept them together despite their stark differences.

"Oh, remember how you were telling me about the Bracewells?" Delia said. "One of them appeared on my doorstep yesterday. It was a bit of a shock."

Marjie gasped. "They didn't threaten you, did they?"

"Oh no," said Delia. "Not exactly. In fact, Elamina was kind of amusing."

Marjie's expression was somewhat unreadable. "Whatever you do, don't trust her." She frowned. "You didn't tell her about the Crone magic, did you?"

"Don't worry," Delia replied. "I didn't show my cards. Something told me not to even ask about the family grimoire until I have more information."

"You're a wise lass," said Marjie reassuringly.

"Speaking of information," Delia added, "I was wondering if it might be useful to hire someone to investigate the Bracewells, see what they can dig up."

Marjie raised an eyebrow in interest. "Do you have anyone in mind?"

"I met a sharp woman the other day called Juniper."

Marjie's expression became even more inscrutable.

"What?" Delia probed.

"Nothing, dear," Marjie replied. "I'm sure Juniper will be effective. Oh, by the way, I've got something for you here." She reached behind the counter and pulled out a bundle wrapped in a bright floral cloth.

"What's that?" Delia asked.

"Just some special charms I've been working on. You know, defensive potions, and so on."

"I'm not really sure how any of that stuff works."

Marjie grinned. "There are plenty of exciting things in here. I borrowed some of Athena's recipes and invented a few of my own – everything from minor explosions to charms that will produce an afternoon tea in a jiffy."

Delia laughed. "That does sound brilliant, actually. Why are you giving them to me?"

Marjie shrugged. "Well, I put some aside for everybody, and I thought you might want something on hand...just in case. My intuition tells me that the Order is close to doing something nefarious again. I'm not sure how. As far as we can tell, the invisibility magic is still holding strong, and they haven't figured out a way through it yet. But you never know."

"I suppose," said Delia, uneasily hoping worries didn't evaporate her good mood.

Just then, a dramatic sound issued forth from her phone.

"I've got to take this," said Delia. "It's Gilly."

"Good. Go on, dear."

Delia sat down at a table to take the call.

"Hello, love. How are you doing?"

"I'm actually all right," said Gilly. "I feel like I'm adjusting to all the changes."

"Wonderful," said Delia. "It is quite a lot to deal with, isn't it?"

"What do you mean?" Gilly asked, somewhat defensively.

Delia frowned, though Gillian couldn't see it. "Moving house and changing jobs, everything else."

"Oh, yes, Mum, that's right."

"What did you think I was asking about?" Delia asked.

"Nothing," said Gilly, keeping her voice a little too light and cheerful. Delia decided it was better to maintain the good terms of their relationship than push her daughter for any further details, though she couldn't shake the feeling she was hiding something.

"Perseus sent over the paperwork," Gilly continued. "He said it should arrive this afternoon."

"Excellent," said Delia. "He does seem quite thorough."

"He's a brilliant man. And the kids can't wait to see you for Christmas."

"You will be there too, won't you?" Delia asked, her voice catching in her throat.

"I'll try to be," said Gilly. "I mean, I expect to be, at least for Christmas dinner."

"I hope that new firm of yours doesn't have you working all through the holidays," said Delia. "That would be quite unfair."

"I'm sure we'll figure it out," Gilly reassured her.

Delia spoke briefly to the grandkids, which was a delight, and then ended the call to find that Marjie had brought over a wonderful tray of scones and a pot of coffee.

By the time she made it back home, she found there was indeed a large envelope on the doorstep filled with legal papers.

"Everything is in order," Delia assured herself, though she could not totally believe it. Despite her good mood that morning her shoulders now ached, and her spine tingled with the threat of danger, especially since the dreaded winter solstice was only one sleep away!

CHAPTER 29
THE SHEPHERD

The first rays of dawn pierced through the frost-etched windows of Father Benedict's chamber. Today was no ordinary day; it was the winter solstice. A day of great significance, not just for the spiritual and celestial realms but also for The Mission that had consumed him for decades. A smug smile curled at the corners of his lips; today was the day he would gain the upper hand.

He rose from his bed, the sheets meticulously folded back as if a spirit of discipline hovered around him even in sleep.

Stepping onto the cold wooden floor, he began his morning exercises. Each push-up, each plank, was a physical manifestation of his lifelong struggle against disorder, chaos, and especially, the witches that were a ceaseless blight on the world.

His routine complete, he dressed in his monastic attire with precision and care. Every fold, every crease in the fabric aligned with the same meticulousness that characterised his strategy room.

A servant entered with a tray, five minutes late, but even this did not ruin the Crimson Shepherd's good mood. He broke his fast with the simple fare – gruel, a slice of coarse bread, and a cup of hot water infused with a single lemon slice. Austere, but sufficient.

Seated there at his table, chewing each bite an appropriate number of times, he pondered on the unpredictable force that was Delia, the fire crone.

Despite years of surveillance, study, and covert manoeuvres, her behavior remained an enigma. But it didn't matter. He had woven a web, intricate and discreet, in just the perfect locale to ensnare her. His trap was set, and he felt the thrill of the hunt surge through his veins.

His meal concluded, he made his way to his strategy room, locking the door behind him. His eyes scanned over the rows of scrolls and the carefully stretched maps, each a small display of his understated genius.

He unfurled a new scroll and began to write, the quill dancing over the parchment with controlled enthusiasm.

It was a final set of instructions for his operatives – precautions, contingencies, but above all, an exhortation to adhere to The Plan.

Just as he was about to roll the scroll closed, a knock came at the door.

"Enter," he barked, brimming with an authority that could

only come from the conviction of imminent victory.

The Cleric stepped in, holding yet another scroll in his shaking hands.

"I bring news, Shepherd," the Cleric stammered, clearly unnerved by the palpable energy in the room.

Father Benedict nodded, indicating that he should continue.

"We have confirmation. The operatives have moved into position. The location has been occupied with the subject, and we are ready for the event."

A victorious smile unfurled across Father Benedict's face. "Very well," he said, savouring the words like a long-awaited meal. "It's time to begin phase two."

He returned to his desk, sealing the newly-written scroll with a drop of crimson wax. The flame of the candle flickered for a moment, as if bowing to his indomitable will. He handed this scroll to the Cleric who bowed and exited, leaving Father Benedict alone in his sanctuary of plans and plots.

Order would prevail. After so many years of dedication, he was but hours away from proving himself.

The strategy room seemed to narrow, echoing back his thoughts in a harmonious chorus of agreement. Yes, the dawn of the winter solstice marked a turning point, not just for the heavens but for his life's work.

And somewhere in that complex web he had spun, Delia would be caught, squirming and powerless. The thought exhilarated him. Today, order would not just prevail; it would triumph!

CHAPTER 30
DELIA

The morning of the winter solstice dawned bright and frosty. Delia stood out the back of her house and took several deep breaths.

Following Marjie's advice, with a bit of her own inspiration thrown in, she focused on visualising flames in her mind and connecting with the element of fire, the heat that ran through her veins, her passion.

"Alright, fiery rage," she said to herself, "you've served me well throughout my life – most of the time, anyway. Now, I just need to get you to *work*."

She opened her eyes, focused on the scrunched-up piece of paper, and imagined bringing her fury bursting to life.

It helped to think of the unfair things, Marjie had said. So Delia thought of how Jerry was treating her, how Gillian hadn't talked to her, barely at all, and how Delia had suddenly put herself and everyone she loved into great danger through no fault of her own. And all of a sudden, the ball of paper burst into flames.

Delia yelped in glee and clapped her hands together, like a tiny child. "I've done it, I've done it!" she exclaimed.

She wasn't sure whether she should call Marjie to celebrate or try again to see if she could hone the power first. Using it predictably and safety was the priority.

Before she could make her decision, the phone rang anyway.

Delia answered it without thinking, without even looking at the screen.

"Hello?"

"Delia."

"Kitty? Umm, I'm kind of in the middle of something right now. Can I call you back?"

"No, Delia. I've been kidnapped." Kitty's voice was hoarse.

"What?"

"These awful people in robes..." Kitty continued. "Terrible really – although some of them are quite handsome...Anyway, they came to my house in the middle of the night, and the next thing I know, I'm on a stage! It's kind of like one of those spicy romance novels, except nothing very interesting has happened yet and I'm afraid I might be in actual danger."

Delia gulped. "What colour robes are they wearing?" she asked.

"Sort of maroon, or some sort of shade of red, I suppose," said Kitty. "Why is that important?"

"That's what I thought," Delia said. "Remember how you said I was paranoid?"

"Oh, I see," said Kitty. "So there was actually somebody after you. Is this some rival theatre troupe?"

"No, well..." Delia contemplated whether she could get away with covering it all up as something mundane, but she was afraid that would only make matters worse later. Besides, how could she possibly explain? "Look, they're very dangerous," she said, deciding that trying to explain magic right now seemed like more trouble than it was worth.

"Well, I gathered that," said Kitty, unimpressed but seemingly taking it all in her stride. "They have a message for you. I told them to call you themselves, but they said it was me who had to do it."

"What's the message?" Delia asked.

"You're to come to the St. Bernard theatre as quickly as possible. If you're not here by the end of the day they...well, it gets a bit vague there actually. I assume they're going to murder or torture me." Kitty giggled.

"Is that funny?" Delia asked. "It sounds dire!"

"You know I can't react properly to serious situations," said Kitty. "And you know I just laugh when I get surprised, and this is a rather surprising situation. I feel like I should be mad at you. You could have warned me. I'd have worn nicer underwear." Kitty cackled at that.

"There'll be plenty of time for that later," Delia reassured.

"Being mad at me, I mean. The underwear seems hardly relevant."

"Pity," said Kitty with a sigh. "I don't really know what else to say. I mean...of course this is some kind of trap."

"Indeed," said Delia, her panic rising further, even though her friend continued to laugh.

"No, I'm still talking," Kitty said. It sounded as if she was trying to wrestle the phone from someone, no doubt someone wearing a crimson hood.

"Anyway," Kitty continued, having clearly won the tussle. "Don't you think it's a trap?"

"Of course it's a trap, Kitty," Delia said. "That doesn't mean I can leave you there."

"Well, exactly," Kitty agreed. "I'd be even madder at you if you did that. So, I think you'd better come. I don't want to be left alone with these guys...unless this turns out like one of those spicy romance novels...and then, well, they'd better buy me a drink first."

Delia couldn't help but laugh at that. Her best friend was such a character, even in the most dire of situations, or perhaps *especially* in the most dire of situations. "I love you, Kitty," said Delia.

"Love you too, DeeDee."

"Don't you dare die on me. I'm gonna figure this out."

"I'm glad you sound confident," said Kitty. "Oh, I've got to go now. They're taking the phone away."

"Get them to offer you that drink," Delia said quickly before the phone cut out.

It was the most terrible and ridiculous of situations. Kitty was right, laughing at the absurdity was not a totally inappropriate response. Although, Delia's own laughter would have been much more maniacal if she hadn't been in more of a screaming mood. It was fortunate that she was still outside, because as she opened her mouth to scream a great burst of flame shot out from the front of her body.

She looked down at her singed clothing and coughed as she brushed away the smoke. "I'm going to have to get something more flame-proof to wear in London," she muttered before laughing, then crying, then hyperventilating.

After a shot of whiskey laced with Marjie's calming potion, she sat down at the kitchen table with a plate of much-needed toast and tried to collect her thoughts.

Her mind felt scattered as if pieces had been strewn across the kitchen floor.

Her best friend had been kidnapped, and it was really Delia's fault; she had put her at risk. It was foolish of her to let Kitty sort out the apartment, and even more foolish not to have warned her off earlier so that she'd never try to visit in the first place.

But Delia knew that blaming herself was not only pointless but also a waste of her energy. The ridiculous group of monks would have found her anyway. They would have tracked down her friends and loved ones, one by one. She was a little surprised that it wasn't Gillian or the children they had targeted. Delia vaguely recalled that the lawyer, Perseus Burk, had muttered something about them being under protection. That was something to be grateful for, at least. It was bad enough having her best friend taken captive, let alone all the family that mattered to her as well.

Delia's first instinct was to call Marjie, but the poor woman already had enough on her mind, what with this being the winter solstice, and everything going on with Rosemary and Athena.

Besides, the last thing Delia needed was for one of the crones to talk her out of going after her friend. She didn't know how ruthless the Order of Crimson was planning to be, but she wasn't keen to test them. For all she knew, they could be riding their fearsome dragons around London by now.

Delia knew that Agatha and Ingrid would try to talk her out of going after Kitty, especially with the solstice ceremony only hours away.

Obviously, it was a terrible idea to walk straight into a trap, but all the options seemed terrible. She wasn't going to wait around all day and go to a winter festival just on the off-chance that the Order might change tact. She thought about calling the London police but decided against it; the risks were too great. What if the Order had spies within the authorities?

Delia's one consolation was that she was still invisible to the members of the Order.

"Being a crone has its perks," she muttered.

Delia carefully strapped several kitchen knives inside her

jacket, and gathered together a bundle of the charms Marjie had made her 'just in case'.

She practiced using her powers one more time, successfully igniting a piece of paper outside. Despite her churning emotions she managed not to set the rest of the garden on fire.

"Nice focus, Spark," she said to herself, trying to provide her own positive reinforcement.

Moments later, she got into her car, ready to drive to the theatre. She didn't exactly have a plan, but she had time to think about one on the way. Part of her questioned whether she might be running away. After all, going back to London was abandoning the crones.

Yet, in reality, she was running directly towards danger, and that was even worse!

CHAPTER 31
MARJIE

Marjie found herself standing in the cosy kitchen of Thorn Manor. She'd been counting down the days to the solstice, but now that it had finally arrived she was rather at a loss as to how to proceed.

The sentient house had graciously cleaned up after her early morning bread-baking endeavours, leaving the countertops immaculate. The scent of yeast and warm dough still lingered in the air, mixing with the aromatic brew of Lady Grey tea she had made earlier. Marjie had been awake since the break of dawn, and her instincts led her towards the kitchen, as usual, baking something calming and simple for Rosemary and Athena, filling the house with these comforting smells.

They wouldn't want a grand breakfast with their underworld journey ahead; simple toast would do, but it would be made from fresh bread baked with love and a little something extra for the nerves.

Marjie knew she should leave the house early. It would give Rosemary and Athena, who were still peacefully ensconced in their beds, some quiet time. The trip to the underworld wasn't something she could assist with, and Agatha said they'd be gone for several days after the solstice if it all worked out. Tension had been rising and Marjie was doing her best to give them space. Today was bound to be incredibly stressful for them, and the least she could do was make herself scarce for a few hours.

The only problem was, she didn't know exactly where to go. She was meeting the other crones later that day, but her shop was closed for the holiday and Papa Jack was busy with his wonderful family.

She picked up her leather handbag, the texture soft yet sturdy beneath her fingers. Her eyes caught a glimpse of the morning light filtering through the vintage lace curtains, casting a soft glow that accentuated the rich colours of the room.

She was ready to leave, though her heart longed to stay with her dear Thorn girls, to care for them, but intuition told her to leave now.

She made her way to the front door, but just as her hand touched the antique brass doorknob, a deep sense of foreboding washed over her. It was as if the air had suddenly thickened, and she could hear her own heartbeat drumming in her ears. Something was drastically wrong.

She could feel it in her bones. It wasn't Rosemary and

Athena; they were still fast asleep in their beds. But something was off, and she couldn't ignore the feeling.

Pulled by a sense of urgency, Marjie dialled Agatha's number, her fingers nervously tapping on the phone.

"Something's not right," she said as soon as Agatha answered.

"Oh, bother you and your irrational intuition," Agatha retorted, her voice dripping strongly with playful scepticism.

"I'm serious, Aggie," Marjie insisted.

Agatha sighed. "If you say so. What is it then?"

"That's the other problem," Marjie admitted, her voice tinged with a mixture of worry and frustration. "I don't know exactly what's wrong."

"That's the problem with intuition," Agatha grumbled. "It's about as useful as a chocolate cauldron and not nearly as delicious."

It was Marjie's turn to sigh. "It's not very specific is it? It could be something to do with that blasted Order of Crimson, but I really have no idea."

"No," Agatha replied, her tone softening. "But we do know someone who can probably figure it out."

"What about Delia?" Marjie asked.

"We'll get her later, as agreed," said Agatha. "Let the girl rest a bit longer – we don't want to overwhelm her with your pesky intuitions."

With that, they decided to go to the woods and pay Ingrid a

visit. If anyone could shed light on the uneasy feeling gnawing at Marjie, it was her.

Marjie quickly changed into a thicker winter coat and boots.

With one last look around the kitchen, as if drawing strength from the space that had provided her so much comfort over the years, Marjie left Thorn Manor.

As she closed the door behind her, the finality of the click echoed in her ears. She couldn't shake the unsettling sensation that their world, as they knew it, was subtly but undeniably shifting.

The cool, crisp air outside filled her lungs as she stepped out into the frosty morning. The sensation of fresh snow crunching beneath her boots was both jarring and comforting, anchoring her to the moment.

Whatever was coming, Marjie knew she wouldn't face it alone.

CHAPTER 32
DELIA

Delia parked a couple of blocks away from the theatre, to preserve the element of surprise and to avoid drawing attention.

As far as she knew, the crone magic was still protecting her from being seen, but she doubted the Order of Crimson would react well to a car approaching with an invisible driver.

Additionally, the walk would give her time to think. Walking had always helped clear her head. Usually, it was pacing back and forth on the stage during rehearsals, but a walk around the block to the theatre would do just as well.

She was well-aware that she was acting without thinking things through. She'd grabbed a few supplies and jumped in the car after receiving the call from her best friend. She'd done the very thing that a character in a play wasn't supposed to do. The infuriating thing! But she couldn't let Kitty be tortured, and she was sure the other Crones would only try to stop her from walking straight into the Order's trap.

Her most important weapon was the element of surprise.

She was invisible...If only she could figure out a way to render Kitty invisible as well, or somehow distract whoever was guarding her. That seemed like a possibility, considering that many of the charms Marjie had given her seemed better suited to creating excellent birthday party decorations or lemon meringue pie than fighting off enemies. She'd rifled through the parcel earlier, raising her eyebrows at several of the charms and questioning what on earth Marjie had been thinking. A handful, though, looked like they might be more effective – apparently, Athena had designed these ones for combat. Rather than worrying about how many witchy teenagers might be out there with a hobby of producing dangerous magical artefacts, Delia chose to be grateful.

She'd shoved a couple of charms in her pockets, ready to throw them at a moment's notice.

First, she needed to scope out the place, look at all the exits, and figure out the most viable escape route.

Her heart was pounding as she neared the theatre building, and it leapt to her throat as a man emerged from the shadows wearing a leather hat.

"Stop," he said quietly. "You don't want to go in there."

"Excuse me?" Delia retorted, narrowing her eyes at him. "Don't you work for the Order? Don't they want me to go in there?"

The man scowled, a gesture that would make most people look unattractive. For him, though, it only accentuated his rugged handsomeness, something that only made Delia glare at him more determinedly.

"I work for myself," he stated gruffly.

"Well, I suspected that you're some sort of magical assassin. But since it doesn't look like you're about to kill me, I'd appreciate it if you let me make my own life choices."

She attempted to sidestep him but found herself pinned against the wall. Not violently, but firmly. It was a move that would have made Kitty's romance heroines swoon, but Delia was not in the mood for it.

"Leave me alone," she said firmly, her rage igniting in her hands. The rogue's sleeve began to smoke. He yelled and stepped back, allowing Delia to dodge past him.

"You'll regret this!" he yelled after her as she sprinted toward the theatre and the impending danger.

CHAPTER 33
THE ROGUE

One hour earlier, Declan had stood at the edge of the forest, its verdant canopy stretching out behind him like a comforting embrace. Magic shimmered around him. Old magic. His magic.

It formed a circle, a picture window into what looked like another world.

His eyes scanned the bustling cityscape. London was a far cry from the mystical serenity of the forest. His heart ached as he felt the nature spirits and energies recede, their gentle melodies replaced by the grating clamour of the city. He knew he had to make this journey, yet every step felt like a betrayal.

His mind was filled with contrary thoughts pulling for his attention. He was burdened by the complexity of his mission for the Order and the arcane contract that restricted his freedom. He could feel the strands of energy chaining him to them. Failure to fulfil his contract would result in the immediate revocation of his magic, an unthinkable fate for an immortal with nothing else to live for.

Yes, the Order had summoned him, but he also knew that Delia Spark was on her way to London. He had told the truth that he could not track her for the purposes of the Order, but they had no idea he'd been keeping close tabs on her for his own purposes, if only he understood exactly what those were.

He took a deep breath, clenched his fists, and stepped into the swirl of energies that would transport him to London.

A dizzying kaleidoscope of colours engulfed him, leaving a residual hum in his magic core. When it cleared, he found himself in an alleyway – a world away from the natural harmony of Myrtlewood. Here, brick and mortar loomed like towering giants, while people moved with frantic energy, their auras blurred and jagged from the pollutants of urban living.

Declan prowled through the backstreets of London, a city he hadn't planned on revisiting again anytime soon.

Yet, here he was, summoned by cryptic messages from the Order of Crimson. His heavy leather boots made little sound on the wet footpath.

The cold, damp morning air was thick with fumes and smog, a grimy mixture that filled his nostrils and coated his tongue. It was a far cry from the earthy fragrances of Myrtlewood's ancient forests, and it made his skin crawl. He missed the simple purity of natural scents: trees, damp earth, the metallic tinge of freshly spilt blood from his hunt. Here, everything was overshadowed by the stench of humanity's vices: greed, power, lust.

His thoughts wandered to the encounters he'd had with Delia Spark. Something about her had awakened long-dormant feelings within him. Feelings that he had no business indulging in. The memory of her gaze, so fierce yet vulnerable, tugged at something inside him. Something he didn't want to examine too closely.

His internal war was interrupted when he sensed her. Delia was near, and she was headed straight into the lair of her enemies.

He felt a surge of jarring concern.

What in all the worlds was she thinking?

The Crone magic unleashed in the abandoned hamlet of Gildea had protected her, but for how much longer? The Order must have pulled some strings to lure her here, but surely she must not be fool enough to fall for their trap.

He moved quickly, positioning himself in the alley adjacent to the theatre where he, too, had been summoned. And then she appeared, as if materialising from the mist itself.

"Stop," he uttered, his voice tinged with an urgency he didn't care to admit. "You don't want to go in there."

"Excuse me?" Her eyes narrowed, and in that moment, Declan felt seen in a way he hadn't in centuries. Delia didn't like him. She didn't want to see him at all, but somehow she did anyway. "Don't you work for the Order? Don't they *want* me to go in there?"

A scowl etched itself onto his face, a natural reaction, but one he almost instantly regretted. "I work for myself," he growled.

His mind screamed at him, telling him he was a fool for even engaging with her. She was clearly mad and her insanity was contagious. She'd been infecting his mind all along. He needed to escape.

"Well, I suspected that you're some sort of magical assassin," she said dismissively. "But since it doesn't look like you're about to kill me, I'd appreciate it if you let me make my own life choices."

She was defiant, strong. Perversely, this made him want to protect her even more.

Before he could collect his thoughts, she tried to sidestep him.

A mix of instinct and folly led him to reach for her. He had to stop her and, without even thinking it through, his arms grabbed her gently, using the wall as leverage. He held her there. Not violently, but enough to know he was serious.

"Leave me alone," she snapped, and then her hands ignited with a blaze of burning heat and flame that singed his sleeve.

Instinctually, he retreated, the acrid smell of burnt oilskin filling his nostrils.

She darted past him, racing toward impending danger.

"You'll regret this!" he called out as she disappeared from view. The words echoed in the empty alley, a harbinger of misfortunes yet to unfold.

He was left standing alone, his fists clenched, his soul a storm of conflicting emotions.

By the old gods and new, he was trapped.

The Order's threads of influence were woven tightly around him. Normally he wouldn't give a damn. A contract was a contract, after all. And yet, there she was, a woman who compelled him to consider something as irrational as morality.

As he turned and made his way back into the shadows, the realisation that he was at a crossroads weighed heavily on him. The once-clear path of his solitary existence was now a bonfire.

The Order might have orchestrated their devious plots, but Declan now saw a more dangerous game unfolding – one he'd thought he'd left behind centuries ago. A game that had, inexplicably, Delia Spark as its wild card.

He felt the slow awakening of something within him, as if a seed of virtue was germinating in the arid soil of his soul. Whatever this was, it was as magical as it was frightening. And with a rueful smile that was swallowed by the night, Declan stepped deeper into the labyrinth of choices that now lay ahead.

CHAPTER 34
DELIA

The first thing that Delia noticed was how unnervingly quiet St. Bernard's theatre was. The doors were open, but there was no one in sight. It certainly wasn't the biggest theatre in London and it was probably just a coincidence that it happened to be *the* theatre where 'the incident' had occurred.

Delia didn't like to think about it, though it had recently haunted her dreams. It was a reason she gave up acting and had eventually moved into directing, after much soul searching and support from Jerry who'd been so sympathetic at the time.

She'd been about to debut in her starring role when it happened, at the height of her performing career, thus far, and in the prime of her thirties.

She'd stepped onto that stage, ready to shine, and the heel of one of the perfect shoes she was wearing gave out.

She tripped and fell flat on her face.

It was painful to think about.

The reviews at the time had stung even more. A simple mistake she'd never been able to recover from.

Since then, she'd been back to this theatre dozens of times, attending plays and directing them, even managing to put the shame and embarrassment out of her mind most of the time.

It struck her as odd, though. Had the Order really been spying on her enough to know? Had they read through old reviews in ancient newspapers and found out about 'the incident'? Perhaps they were trying to make her feel vulnerable.

At this time of day, on a Saturday, St. Bernard's would normally be humming with life, with the staff and cast popping in and out, getting ready for the evening's performance. That was unnerving in itself. They must have booked the theatre out; they must have been planning this kidnapping well in advance.

Delia suppressed a shudder.

She had no idea really, about these enemies, how powerful they were, how many there were, how much danger they posed.

A small consolation was that they apparently couldn't see her at all. Though that hadn't stopped the cowboy from trying to stop her from coming in. Was that also a ruse to throw her off her game, to confuse her?

Had he already notified them that she was on her way? If he worked for himself, that didn't mean he wasn't contracted by them.

She hesitated halfway through the foyer. There was still nobody in sight.

She almost longed for the sight of cursed red-clad Order guards at the door to the main chamber. The emptiness was eerie.

The main theatre was wide open.

She crept in, slowly, trying to be quiet, even though the invisibility spell should also cloak the sound she made.

She looked across the rows of seating, the red velvet sorely in need of re-upholstery, and up to the bright light ahead. The more lavish velveteen of the red drapes was obscured by the spotlight onstage.

As her eyes adjusted to the light she suppressed a gasp.

Sitting directly below it was a chair, and on that chair was Kitty's crumpled form.

CHAPTER 35
AGATHA

Agatha trudged alongside Marjie through the dense forest, and each step filled Agatha's nostrils with a mixture of damp earth and decaying leaves. Her mind took in all the data of her senses. The wind swished through the towering trees, carrying a concoction of scents – moss, wet wood, and a hint of something she couldn't quite place.

She glanced at Marjie to find her expression was serious, heavy, not the usual rosy smile. This irked Agatha more than she'd like to admit, but some playful insults and banter would surely lighten the mood.

"You know, Marjie, if you didn't walk like a tortoise, we might actually get there," Agatha quipped.

Marjie chuckled, her eyes twinkling. "Oh, darling, speed is for those who have something to run from. I'm not running from my own over-active brain."

Agatha rolled her eyes but couldn't suppress a smile. "If only you had one."

"You know, Agatha, you might find life less vexing if you stopped to smell the roses," Marjie said, a twinkle in her eye.

"Roses? In this forest? The only thing I smell is your over-applied lavender oil."

Marjie chortled. "Well, some of us care about personal presentation."

"In that case, you missed a spot," Agatha retorted, pointing vaguely at her companion's face.

Marjie laughed, clearly enjoying the trading of insults. Just as she opened her mouth for another barbed comeback, the door of Ingrid's hut flew open with such force it nearly unhinged.

Ingrid stood there, narrowing her eyes in suspicion. "You're early!"

Agatha shrugged, taking in the forest witch's powerful presence and tangled hair. "And you're a vision of order, as always."

Ingrid snorted and ushered them in.

The interior of the hut was an overwhelming mix of herbs, incense, and something distinctly feline. The humble home was as warm and inviting as its owner was gruff. Bundles of herbs and talismans lined the walls, casting soft glows that played tricks with the shadows. A kettle hanging over the fire was already on the boil. "Tea?" Ingrid offered.

"As if you need to ask," Marjie replied, settling down at the wooden table.

Agatha sniffed the air as she took her seat. The comforting

woody aroma of the hut mingled with the mustiness of old books and dried herbs.

"Sage and thyme," Ingrid announced, placing teacups in front of them. She poured the tea and took her place at the head of the table.

"Something is dreadfully wrong," Marjie finally said, breaking the silence.

Agatha's eyes rolled dramatically. "You make it sound like we're in a bad melodrama. What's next? Shall we consult the spirits with a Ouija board like teenagers with cheap wine?"

Ingrid's eyes met Marjie's. "I sensed it too. The forest whispered of a new darkness."

Agatha slapped her hand on the table, rattling the teacups. "Oh for heaven's sake, you two. 'Something is dreadfully wrong'? 'A new darkness'? What are we, characters in a second-rate gothic novel?"

"Really Aggie—" Marjie began, but Agatha's rage was already at boiling point.

She slammed her cup down, spilling some tea. "You're both as clear as a cauldron of mud. We need details, facts, data, and analysis. We need clarity. Not woo-woo ominous feelings. And I've told you not to call me Aggie unless I'm drunk."

Marjie shrugged and muttered something under her breath about Agatha always being drunk.

Ingrid snapped back, "Well, aren't we a font of rationality today? Maybe we should've invited Delia. Even that novice crone might offer more usefulness than your incessant griping."

Marjie shrugged with a consoling smile. "Ingrid has a point. You're hardly being useful yourself, Agatha."

Before Agatha could retort, the back door creaked open. In sauntered Mephistos, the cursed cat, his fur bristling with self-importance. "I thought I might find you lot here." He preened before jumping onto the empty chair.

Ingrid shot him a venomous look. "Can't you see we're in the middle of something crucial here? Or does that cursed noggin of yours only comprehend bird-watching and naps?"

"Yes, can't you see we're busy playing tea party with the universe's vague forewarnings?" Agatha snapped.

"I can see that you're in the middle of sitting around, drinking tea, and accomplishing nothing," Mephistos purred.

Marjie shot him a reproachful look. "Tea is not nothing," she muttered.

"As it happens," Mephistos began, jumping onto the table with feline grace and making himself comfortable, "I have some *intelligence.*"

Agatha's nostrils flared. "Speak, cat. Your theatrics waste time."

Mephistos shot her a condescending look. "I've been watching over the Order of Crimson's encampment. There's been significant movement. They're plotting."

"At last, some hard evidence," Agatha said, her face lighting up as she smirked triumphantly at the other witches.

Marjie chuckled. "Oh, Agatha, you and your love affair with 'evidence'! You'd marry a fact if it proposed."

"So tell us," Ingrid demanded, staring at Mephistos. "What is this plan?"

Mephistos licked his paw nonchalantly. "They're targeting the Crones' vulnerabilities. The Order is quite secretive. Even those members I was spying on seem to know very little. But there's movement. In several directions. I'm unsure of the specifics."

"Movement? Bad feelings? That's all you have to offer?" Agatha fumed. "This is unacceptable! I could find more helpful insights in a daily horoscope!"

Mephistos grinned. "Sometimes, all you need to solve a riddle is to count."

"Count?" Ingrid's eyes narrowed, "Count what?"

"One, two, three..." Mephistos' tail swished from side to side.

Agatha sighed, exasperated. "If this is some cryptic feline form of guidance, I—"

Ingrid narrowed her eyes. "See what?"

"There should be four," Mephistos said, plainly.

Marjie sighed. "Delia is at home. She's meeting us soon."

"Is she, now?" Mephistos continued.

Marjie gasped and her face drained of colour. "Oh no! Not Delia!"

Ingrid stood so abruptly her chair toppled over. "Nonsense. The invisibility magic is still powerful. I can sense it. Delia is vulnerable, yes, but she's also protected here."

Mephistos' eyes narrowed into slits. "I wouldn't be so sure about that."

"Stop being so smarmy and cryptic," Marjie instructed. "What are you getting at?"

Mephistos cocked his head. "If I were the Order, the newest arrival in Myrtlewood would be my target. Someone fresh to the magical world with no mastery. Someone with strong connections to loved ones outside the protections of this town."

The room was thick with tension at the severity of the situation. Agatha's mind raced. Could it be a diversion? Could the cursed cat be trusted? Could the real target be something, or someone else? The sensory overload of the hut – its odours and ancient creaks – suddenly became too much. "Enough of this nebulous nonsense," she said with a brittle tone. "If we're to defend ourselves and protect Delia, we need clear plans, corroborated facts, and actionable intelligence. We tighten the protective circles around Delia. We set guards, traps, whatever is necessary. But we also need to dig deeper into the Order's plans. Not just scout and make vague observations. I want names, locations, motives."

Mephistos chuckled softly. "Well, well, someone woke up on the strategic side of the bed today."

Ingrid looked from Marjie to Agatha. "You might be onto something, Agatha. Even a broken clock is right twice a day, but surely this can all wait until after the solstice."

"I fear we're already too late," Marjie interjected, holding her hand to her heart. "That must be it...I tried to call Delia earlier but she didn't answer her phone. I assumed she was having a lie in, but what if the Order drew her out?"

"How?!" Ingrid demanded. "Delia is hot-headed but she's not a total fool."

"She cares deeply about her loved ones," Marjie pointed out. "That's all it would take."

"She'd just leave, willingly, without telling us?!" Agatha thundered. "Irrational!"

Marjie shrugged. "Wouldn't we try to stop her? Wouldn't we tell her to wait until after the solstice at least?"

Ingrid sighed deeply.

In the silence that followed, all three Crones knew that the idle time for talk had passed. Action was needed, and it was needed now. And as much as Agatha loathed to admit it, feelings, vagueness, and all, had their place. But so did action, facts, and clarity, and it was time to blend the two to protect their own.

Mephistos grinned. "Ah, the drama, the suspense! I'll fetch my popcorn."

Agatha shot him a withering look. "It's time for little fluffy to leave. We have work to do."

CHAPTER 36
DELIA

K*itty!*
As if in response to Delia's swirling terrified thoughts, Kitty sighed and changed position slightly.

Delia almost crowed with relief, then held back a giggle as she recognised her best friend's absolutely-bored-senseless posture. Kitty was not someone to drag along to tiresome meetings, and apparently this kidnapping was just as uninspiring.

Delia looked around furtively. Still no sign of the Order.

Aware that she was most definitely walking into a carefully orchestrated trap, she stepped slowly and confidently, more confidently than she felt anyway, up the centre aisle, keeping her breath level, keeping her eyes peeled as her footsteps echoed up towards the stage.

Kitty noticed the sound. As she turned to her, Delia raised a finger to her lips.

Kitty squinted under the light. "Who's there?" she called out.

Delia's heart sank even as it pounded violently in her chest. She had to think first. If Kitty recognised her, it would alert the Order of her presence. She heard a rustling from behind the open curtains.

"Kitty, it's me. But please don't say anything."

Kitty's eyes widened but she didn't speak.

"Don't say anything at all," Delia continued. "Just listen to what I have to say. Alright? Nothing at all." Kitty nodded slowly.

Delia's mind raced, unsure of what to reveal to her friend. The whole situation was so bizarre that she couldn't think of how to explain it without sounding like a raving lunatic.

"You might not believe any of this because it sounds utterly bonkers. This is all new to me too. If you want to reply, pretend that you're talking to them."

Kitty looked around. "Water!" she called out. "I'm parched. Can someone bring me some water?"

There was silence for a moment, and then a shuffling sound. A man in a red cape appeared, striding to the middle of the stage cautiously and handed Kitty a glass of water.

He stared around at the theatre, his eyes brushing straight past Delia.

Invisibility sure had its benefits.

Kitty gulped the water down. "Now can you tell me what the hell I'm doing here?"

The man looked around, shrugged, and muttered something

about checking with his superior. Clearly, he was an underdog and not qualified to speak.

"I don't have a solid plan for how to get us out of here," Delia said, "but I do have some ridiculous magic in my bag that can probably create one heck of a distraction. Then maybe we can sneak out."

"Can somebody explain to me," Kitty cried dramatically, "why it is that I'm here? And why Delia has to get on the stage? How does this all make sense in your plan?"

Kitty was clearly trying to communicate something, though Delia had no idea what he was on about.

"You strange robed men want Delia on stage, right?" Kitty continued. "What does it have to do with this blue circle of salt that you sprinkled around me?" she asked with theatrical waves of her hand.

Kitty was trying to give Delia information about the kind of trap the Order had laid. She was tied to the chair; her arms were free, perhaps to aid her in the drinking of water. But she clearly could not reach the fastenings, and even if she tried, the Order would be on her before she had the chance.

Delia's mind swirled in panic. Her power was not honed enough that she could set the rope on fire and release her friend without potentially burning her to a crisp and, granted, setting the entire building on fire. It was too much of a risk.

Delia needed to get up there, but it seemed that crossing that circle of blue salt would be a terrible idea.

She heard footsteps and the same henchman came back on

stage.

"Please stop asking questions," he mumbled. "You're not supposed to know about the plan."

"Well, I wouldn't know about it at all if you didn't keep talking about it," Kitty shot back. "By the way, Delia is not coming," she announced. "I used a special code when I talked to her on the phone. The code means that I was simply making up stories in the bedroom with my new boyfriend, and Delia thinks this is all part of one of our games."

Delia suppressed a laugh at the silly nonsense her friend was making up. She really did have a wild imagination.

Kitty waggled her eyebrows suggestively at the guard. "So unless you intend on becoming my new boyfriend, I suggest you untie me and end this outrageous charade."

The henchman blushed the same shade as his robe and mumbled something indecipherable before shuffling off stage again.

"I'm doing my best here," Kitty called out after him.

"I know you are," said Delia. "The problem is that I can't think of any other way that I can release you that doesn't involve me getting on stage. I might just have to set up the distraction and barge in anyway."

Kitty slumped forward. "I am very uncomfortable here," she said. "Please release me."

"I can't do that," the henchman called from behind the curtain. "Just be quiet for a minute. We're waiting for her to arrive."

"She's not coming," Kitty insisted. "She obviously doesn't care about me enough anyway." She winked.

"What was that?" the henchman asked.

"I was merely winking at you," she called back. "You know, I quite like foot rubs with lots of oil," she said with a flirtatious voice, making Delia giggle.

This invisibility spell was a hell of a blessing.

Delia tiptoed around the side of the stage, towards the fire exit towards at back of the building.

She could see guards huddled behind the curtains, hiding – no doubt waiting to pounce on her when she made her grand entrance. Perhaps they didn't understand enough about the invisibility spell, or at least that was what Delia's wishful thinking told her. But why weren't they guarding the side entrances?

Delia didn't have time to think. She reached into her bag and pulled out the bundle of charms that Marjie had given her, knowing that most of them could be set off by throwing them. Holding the bundle high up in the air, Delia was distinctly aware that this wasn't exactly what Marjie had in mind, but she hurled it with as much force as she could muster towards the fire door, sending a blast of flame behind it.

A puff of sparkling smoke burst into the air.

"What's that?" a guard cried.

"Over there." Another pointed towards the door.

By this time, Delia had already retreated back to the centre of the room. She couldn't help but turn back to see a throng of red-hooded men bamboozled by glitter, small brightly coloured explosions, and even lemon meringue pie to the face.

"Amazing," she muttered, dashing up towards the stage.

There was nothing for it.

As she lurched past the salt barrier she felt a popping sensation and then a swelling wave which receded with a tearing pain. The invisibility magic had been broken. With a stab of guilt, she pulled out her kitchen knife and began cutting Kitty's bonds. Delia may have just betrayed the Crones but saving Kitty was more important.

"Thank God," said Kitty.

"I'm not sure if he's the one you should be thanking," said Delia. "Though I hear there are a whole lot of gods and goddesses that are actually real."

"Whatever," said Kitty. "Just get me out of here. This place is dreadfully boring!"

No sooner had she cut through the first rope than a sound echoed across the stage.

From the opposite direction of the commotion came slow clapping. Brighter lights beamed on, illuminating the entire stage and blinding Delia.

She held up her hand to shield her eyes and looked across.

"I suppose you can see me now," she said to the figure in the bright, crimson hooded cloak which looked to be made of silk velvet rather than felt.

"That's the idea," said a familiar voice. Delia felt a shadow of shock hit her.

CHAPTER 37
THE SHEPHERD

Two hours earlier, Father Benedict settled into the backseat of the motor car. The smooth leather exuded a warmth that wrapped around him, a tactile assurance that his path ahead was righteous.

He looked out the tinted windows and watched the countryside blur into a swirl of colours – green fields dotted with quaint cottages, clusters of sheep grazing under the scattered sunbeams that broke through the clouds.

A gentle drizzle had started, and the soft patter of raindrops on the roof played a rhythm that intermingled with the distant hymns that wafted into his thoughts.

The motor hummed softly; a mechanical beast glided as if guided by the hand of the Almighty, ferrying him to a moment that had been foretold.

The revelation.

The odour of the plush car interior – a mixture of leather, polish, and the musky cologne of his driver – filled the enclosed space. He felt it in his bones; this journey was as much a pilgrimage as it was a mission.

The powers of the Almighty had guided him here, to this very moment. Every move was choreographed, and he, a gracious dancer performing his lead role, was fulfilling his purpose on earth: to restore justice and honour to the world.

His fingers tapped the amulet that hung from his neck – a sacred and consecrated relic and a symbol of his hard-fought triumphs.

It had been several months since his extended fieldwork had ended, several months cloistered back in the compound of the Order of Crimson.

Every moment had been spent meticulously working, with tireless but understated vigour, to restore dignity to the Order and to set the strategy and operations of The Mission into motion.

His underlings might be bumbling buffoons, but even their mishaps were guided by an all-seeing holy presence.

Father Benedict's breath stilled as his thoughts brushed against the treasured memory: that very presence that he had glimpsed once, many years before he'd earned his title as the Crimson Shepherd. That singular vision had set the course for his entire life, a path that he'd followed with grim determination and humble sacrifices that were far greater than any other in the Order.

The memory of that day swelled in his mind, casting a divine glow over the landscapes he passed.

He could still feel the ineffable touch of something greater, something that had sent him on this mission with a driving passion. The presence had whispered secrets to him, divine truths that separated him from the others, that made him the chosen shepherd to lead his flock through the trials and tribulations of the temporal world.

There was only one way toward the greater good. Only one right way of thinking, of being, and Father Benedict did his utmost to exemplify this in every single aspect of his living, even deep in the field where his morals could have easily been sullied if he were a lesser mortal.

Now, as the car approached the outskirts of London – the towering buildings of the metropolis poking through the misty haze like sentinels – he felt a rush of divine energy course through him. It was as if the Almighty Himself had breathed life into his cells, confirming his destined path.

The brimstone taint in the air told him that the evil forces were already gathering, their putrid smell mixing with the city's natural stench of diesel and fast food.

He clenched his hands, drawing strength from his own resolve. His mind raced with calculations, each thought a component in a grand equation that would soon reach its solution. The Crones had no idea what was coming, no inkling of the storm that would sweep away their lives, leaving them bereft and broken. Their ignorance was their weakness, and their weakness was his opportunity.

As the car pulled into a secluded alley, he took a deep breath. The scent of wet cobblestones and rusting metal greeted him.

The door opened, and Father Benedict stepped onto the uneven pavement. His leather shoes tapped with authority as he walked into a nondescript building. The poorly lit interior, scented with the smell of stale tobacco and old wood, seemed to bow in his presence. His footsteps on the creaky floorboards were like pronouncements, each one declaring his intent to the world.

He was the Crimson Shepherd, and he was about to usher in a new era. One where justice and honour reigned supreme, where the scourge of the unworthy would be eradicated once and for all. It all began with seizing the ancient powers of the Myrtlewood Crones, and for that, he was ready.

It was time for the revelation.

It was time to destroy Delia Spark.

CHAPTER 38
DELIA

She snapped back from where she was helping Kitty up towards the man.

Delia was swept up in a storm of shock which ricocheted through her entire body.

"You!" she said.

His hood slipped back to reveal none other than the face of the man she'd spent thirty years of her life with...the man she'd been fighting in divorce, who had gone from being her confidant and partner to being her enemy, apparently in more ways than one.

"Jerry," she said with distain.

He did not bother acknowledging her by name.

Kitty looked from Delia to Jerry and decided to hold her tongue for once, though Delia could tell she had a lot of coarse words at the ready by the rage showing on her face.

"What the hell are you doing here?" Her voice was thick with revulsion.

"Oh, you have no idea how long I've waited for this moment," Jerry said in his excited voice, the one he only used when dreaming up a big production, or right before a show.

Delia now understood the full experience of the rug being pulled from beneath her.

"What do you mean?" She narrowed her eyes. "I take it you're involved with this revolting cult. Did they rope you into it? Did they promise you something? Did they threaten you or did you just join in voluntarily in order to humiliate me?"

"Far from it," said Jerry. "In fact, I was born into the Order, just like my father and my grandfather before him."

Delia scoffed. "How exactly is one born into a cult that seems comprised entirely of men, Jerry?"

"It's not a cult," he replied. "And don't call me Jerry. Not anymore. My name is Jeremiah Benedict Venito. You may call me by my title, the Crimson Shepherd." His eyes gleamed with malice. "A title I earned through decades in the field."

"That's an interesting thing to call our sham of a marriage," Delia said, rolling her eyes.

Jerry – because Delia refused to call him by a ridiculous title – glared at her. "You always were hot-headed."

Kitty barked out a laugh. "And you were always an arrogant fu—"

"Kitty," Delia cut in.

Kitty mimed zipping her mouth closed. And then mumbled, "He didn't even answer your question."

"That's true," said Delia. "Maybe he's too embarrassed to explain the circumstances of his birth."

Jerry's face grew red, as it often did in anger. "I will be the one asking questions!" he blustered. "And for your information, it is tradition in the Order for men of age to go out into the world and beget children. The boys return to the Order at seven years of age. That is how it has always been done, for centuries."

"What a batshit crazy cult." Kitty was no longer trying to remain quiet.

Delia wrinkled her nose in disgust. "You told me your upbringing was strict and old-fashioned, but this is one step too far. We were married for what? Thirty years?"

"Thirty-four years, seven months, and twelve days," said Jerry.

"I'm surprised you weren't counting down the seconds." Delia raised a hand to her face, rubbing her temple to help all this sink in. "I knew our marriage was a sham, but I didn't realise it was so deliberate. I can't quite believe it...Surely you're making this up and it's a ploy by the Order to distract me."

"How dare you question my legitimacy!" Jerry roared. "It was my mission. I'd studied you from afar. Our oracle told us that you were to be one of the demon women, and I took it upon myself to seduce you. I shaped our life together to keep you firmly under control until the time was right."

"Revolting," said Delia. "We have a child."

"Fortunately not a boy child," Kitty muttered. "No wonder he and Gilly were never close."

"An unintended consequence," said Jerry with disdain.

Delia felt the weight of guilt and shame crashing into her. It wasn't just her marriage that was a sham. It was Gilly's whole childhood. "You were a pretty awful father, you know that?"

Jerry's face returned to his usual calm, calculated expression. "I should have had a son. All the men in my family breed heirs. However, I believe this was a test from the Almighty. He was making sure I was a worthy disciple."

Delia's rage was almost burning a hole in her chest. "How can you stand there all pious when you were carrying on with all those mistresses?"

Jerry's expression went cold. "More futile attempts to produce an heir. I can assure you, I did not enjoy a single moment. The Almighty was testing me still, until I learned my lesson. I am the ultimate heir in His image."

Delia held back a wave of revulsion. "I knew you were religious. But this is a whole other level of extreme fundamentalism."

"I'm pretty sure Gillian is better than any of the men in your family put together," Kitty added.

"A disappointment, just like you," Jerry said. "At every turn, you've thwarted me with your irrational, unpredictable demon woman ways. And finally, I have you exactly where I want you."

Delia looked around at the stage. "It was you, wasn't it? You were the one who ruined my acting career. You were the one who picked up the pieces."

Jerry shrugged nonchalantly. "I might have planted a faulty stiletto. I had been trying to woo you, but you resisted. I got involved in the theatre because I take my dedication to the Almighty seriously. I was a production assistant, but you hardly looked twice at me. That night, your big debut on this stage...It was a brilliant opportunity."

"You call the most embarrassing moment of my life a brilliant opportunity?" Delia's shock was quickly turning to rage, burning so strongly that she was only vaguely aware that she was at risk of setting the entire theatre on fire and burning them all to a crisp.

"I needed to break you down, you see." Jerry's eyes flashed with his own arrogance. "I needed you to feel weak and humbled. You were far too strong for your own good. Not that it made any difference in the long term. You insisted on being a director, so I went along with it."

"We were a team..." said Delia. "And now I realise that you actually were undermining me that entire time."

"It served its purpose," said Jerry. "I was trying to keep you busy, keep you away from that godforsaken village of witches and fools. We need to take back that power. Women should know their place. They should serve men; it is as the Almighty intended."

Kitty let out a stream of expletives so extreme that in any other circumstance they might be shocking.

"That's just about the most absurd thing I've ever heard, *Jerry*," said Delia. "You're a sad little man with a sad little cult. Now, if you're quite finished with your evil mastermind rant, I'm busting Kitty out of here and you'd better get out of my way."

She spoke a tough game for somebody with only kitchen knives as weapons and an unpredictable furnace. She wasn't afraid to use fire against this man whom she'd once trusted but who had revealed himself to be an even worse manipulator than she'd already realised him to be. She would set him alight right then and there, but the theatre was mostly comprised of wood and synthetic velvet. Delia's magic seemed to protect her from her own flames but she couldn't risk Kitty's life.

"You won't be leaving this building until I say you will," said Jerry, trembling with rage in his voice. "And you will now address me as 'Master'," he added.

Delia threw back her head and laughed, and so did Kitty. They were practically falling over each other in hysterics.

Jerry's whole body shook, his face turning bright red, and that vein popping out of his head the way that it tended to do when he really lost his cool.

"Enough!" he cried, barking the word in fury.

"You know, I think we *have* had enough," said Delia, wiping tears of laughter from her eyes.

"Guards!" Jerry commanded.

Delia pulled Kitty up and they scrambled towards the steps leading from the stage, heading towards the opposite fire exit, but they quickly found themselves surrounded.

"You have no escape," Jerry's voice boomed. "Now that you've walked into our trap, we can see you. You're no longer protected by that blasted magic. The Order can seek you out, you and the other evil that you work with, your mistresses."

"Steady on," said Delia. "We don't even have a leader."

Kitty chuckled. "I don't know why, but this situation, despite the danger, is the most absurd I've ever been in."

Delia patted her on the shoulder, trying to still her own racing heartbeat and come up with a plan.

Jerry continued, "Now that we know the locations of all the evil crones, we can unleash the beasts that hold the ancient power, in line with our birthright and the sacred purpose of the Order."

Kitty sighed. "This is decidedly unsexy," she complained.

"Stop speaking," Jerry called, clearly unimpressed with not being taken seriously. "Gag her," he cried out.

The Order guards surrounding Delia and Kitty shuffled forward, hesitantly. Delia wasn't sure if it was because they were scary women or because of her magic, but the guards were clearly unsure of how to seize and gag them. Still, she and Kitty were clearly outnumbered.

Delia's heart hammered and her brain tried desperately to think of an escape. Was blasting them to fiery smithereens worth risking Kitty's safety?

"Now!" Jerry commanded, and the guards reached forward.

"I think not," came a stern and raspy voice from the back of the hall.

Delia recognised Ingrid at once and breathed a sigh of relief.

"You brought reinforcements. This is unacceptable!" Jerry sounded as if he was telling off a naughty child.

"I think you'll find crones reinforce themselves," said another voice, coming from a different direction entirely. This time it was Marjie speaking. And though Delia couldn't see her, as the other Crones were clearly using their own cloaking magic, she felt infinitely safer just knowing she was there.

"Evil women! You're outnumbered," Jerry cried, raising his hand in the air.

"I think we've had about enough of his voice for today, don't you?" said Agatha's voice, and an apple drifted through the air and wedged itself in Jerry's open mouth. His muffled rage was almost as hilarious as the sight of him struggling against a piece of fruit.

The Order members looked around in confusion as a thick, dense black fog fell across the room.

Delia could barely see anything. She held tight to Kitty as friendly hands reached out for them, pulling them through the darkness and elbowing guards out of their path.

"I think the front door's the best bet," said Agatha.

"They did leave it wide open," said Marjie. "Come on, let's go!"

It was dark, so dark, as they walked through the thick fog created by the Crones. Delia felt cared for and safe in that darkness. Never had she been more grateful that magic existed than she was right then in that moment. Around them, muffled sounds of confusion echoed amid shouts of anger and rage that grew more and more distant as they made their way through the main doors of the theatre and out into the street. The fog cleared, though the sky was naturally darkening.

"Thank you so much," said Delia, her gratitude warring with the acute sense of guilt she felt at running off to save her friend without telling them, and inadvertently destroying the invisibility magic protecting the Crones and the whole town of Myrtlewood in the process.

"We wouldn't leave one of our own to fight alone," said Marjie.

Agatha eyed her warily. "It wasn't a very rational thing to do," she grumbled.

"I should have said something," Delia admitted. "But I was scared you'd stop me and I couldn't leave Kitty there. Now I'm afraid I've put us all in a lot more danger."

Ingrid shrugged. "What's life without a little danger?" Her voice was nonchalant as they strode away from the theatre, but her eyes held a glimmer of concern. Delia looked around, but there were no Order members in sight.

"That must have been quite a shock," said Marjie, patting Delia on the shoulder. "How are you holding up?"

"What?" said Delia. "Oh you mean about the man I thought was my husband secretly just being in some kind of cult and marrying me as part of his mission? Honestly, I don't think it's sunk in yet. It might take me some time to process."

"Fair enough," said Agatha, and Delia noticed her shoulders

relax, just a tad. Perhaps it was a logical enough explanation to set Agatha at ease.

"How did you even find me?"

"It was pretty obvious where you'd gone," said Marjie. "We called in at your house and found the address that you'd written down."

"I suppose I didn't even need to write that down, I know this theatre so well," said Delia. "Although, with my sense of direction, an address is probably a good idea."

"And several mapping systems," Marjie added.

"We all have our faults," Agatha said reassuringly.

"And who are all these people?" said Kitty, looking both appalled and impressed.

"These are my new friends," said Delia.

Kitty's face broke into a wry grin. "Something tells me we're going to get along just fine."

CHAPTER 39
'INGRID

I ngrid gripped the dash, white knuckled with adrenaline as Agatha's car hurtled through the streets. She shot Agatha a sideways glance. "We're either going to break the sound barrier or die trying."

The speedometer's needle was so far into the red it seemed to flirt with the impossibility of turning back. Agatha held the wheel with one hand while her other hand danced in the air, conjuring tendrils of magic that fed into the car's already manic speed.

The magically-enhanced car roared out towards the countryside and through patches of forest, its interior as roomy as a school bus thanks to Agatha's wizardry.

"Given the circumstances, either would be an acceptable outcome," Agatha retorted, a mischievous glint in her eye as she summoned another burst of speed. The car responded as though alive, its growl becoming a near-roar.

Kitty's voice wavered from the back seat. "I thought witches flew on broomsticks, not lead-footed it in rocket cars."

Marjie chortled at the mention of broomsticks.

"Don't you start," Ingrid snapped. It was bad enough the poor newcomer had been thrown into the deep end as far as magic was concerned. The last thing she needed to know right now was exactly how witches traditionally used broomsticks.

"Let's just say we modernised," Agatha responded, her voice tinged with a sardonic humour. "Broomsticks are so last century."

Ingrid withdrew her hands from the dashboard and tried to relax, but a moment later Agatha hit a bump in the road and Ingrid clenched her fists, her nails almost piercing her own skin.

"Agatha, for the love of all that is sacred, slow down!"

She could feel every vibration of the car, every pebble on the road.

The scents of leather and Agatha's singeing magical energy filled her nostrils, each fighting for dominance.

As the car tore through the streets, the countryside became a green-brown blur, rushing by so quickly that it was almost hypnotic. The roar of the wind melded with the growl of the car's engine, and Ingrid felt as though they were caught in some sort of elemental maelstrom.

In the rear view mirror, Ingrid caught a glimpse of Delia, her expression dangerously blank. The poor woman had just been delivered the mother of all revelations. She surely must be reeling at the thought that her decades-long marriage had been a lie orchestrated by a manipulative cult.

Ingrid shuddered.

She'd seen a lot of corruption and shock in her time, but still it was hard to imagine what Delia must be going through.

Beside her, Kitty's eyes were wide as saucers and her face was pale.

"Don't worry, Kitty. Agatha's a pro at reckless driving," Delia said.

"That's...comforting," Kitty squeaked and then broke into raucous laughter.

"Don't mind her," said Delia. "This is how Kitty reacts to danger."

Despite the giggling coming from the back, the tension was palpable, like a spell gone wrong, or a cauldron about to boil over. Each of them was locked in their own thoughts, haunted by what they'd heard in the theatre, and what they still didn't know.

If the Order would go to such extreme lengths over so many years, perhaps even their seemingly bumbling incompetence was orchestrated. It was a common tool used by politicians. Ingrid remembered it from when she used to pay attention to such things. People could easily underestimate a fool. There was almost a charmingly innocent quality to their lack of poise, a relatability in their silliness. It could all be an act, to derail people from their calculated and devious manoeuvrings. Ingrid was unsure how much of the Order of Crimson's actions so far had been cunning strategy rather than blatant foolishness, but it was certain that the Crones had underestimated them. And that was a frightening thought.

Her thoughts drifted back to the darkness she'd seen in the messages from the forest.

"The forest's whispers are getting darker. The kidnapping was only the beginning," Ingrid said.

"I told you. We need to hurry," Agatha replied, sending out another burst of magic.

"And we're vulnerable—"

"We're always vulnerable; that's what makes us strong," said Marjie.

"Rubbish," Agatha grumbled.

Delia interjected, "Agatha's right. We could use a bit less philosophy and a bit more speed, if that's even possible."

"It's always possible," Agatha retorted, adding another dollop of magic to the already unstable mix. The car surged forward, as if propelled by the winds of destiny.

Everyone in the car felt it – a tingling at the base of their spines, a quickening of their heartbeats. They were fast approaching Myrtlewood.

The air inside the car seemed to thicken, filled with shared yet unspoken dread. Each of the Crones knew the winter solstice would be a tipping point. Towards what, they couldn't be sure.

Agatha navigated a sharp turn, the tires squealing in protest.

"Hang on," she muttered, as though the hardest part of their journey was yet to come.

Ingrid gripped her seat tighter, her thoughts racing faster than the speeding car. She no longer compelled Agatha to slow down. It was a desperate race against time, the forest now a dark blur, the dashboard clock ticking away the minutes and seconds. The solstice festivities would be kicking off and then the ritual would begin summoning the energy of this season so potent for all crones. The mysteries ahead were unclear, but the path would be revealed if they trusted it enough to take the first step, of that Ingrid was sure.

"Here we go," Agatha declared as the Mini roared down the road. The car seemed to sense their urgency, the magical engine responding with an almost sentient eagerness.

Agatha's eyes narrowed as she focused on the road ahead, her fingers drumming a quick rhythm on the wheel. They were drawing closer now.

Ingrid sensed Agatha's concentration deepen, felt the thread of magic emanating from her hands intensify, merging with the car's mechanical heart. The boundary between witch and machine was blurring in a dangerous, exhilarating dance.

Marjie chuckled from the back seat. "If I didn't know better, I'd think this old banger has a life of its own."

Agatha shot back, "She does, and don't call her old. We're both in our prime."

Marjie shot back, "If this is what prime looks like, I'm terrified of the decline."

Agatha rolled her eyes. "You haven't even seen my second gear."

Ingrid felt the tension alleviate for just a second, everyone's spirits momentarily buoyed by the ridiculous banter. But underlying it all was the palpable sense of urgency.

She looked over at Agatha, her friend's eyes like twin flames in the dimming light, reflections of unspoken fears and unbreakable resolve. It was a look Ingrid knew well, had seen mirrored in her own eyes on countless occasions. It said: We must not fail.

"We won't," Ingrid whispered, more to herself than anyone else. Agatha glanced at her, a silent nod acknowledging the vow they'd both silently made.

Through the towering trees, Ingrid began to make out the glow of Myrtlewood, the lights shimmering like a distant mirage. It was as if the town itself was calling to them, beckoning them closer with a spectral hand.

"Almost there," Agatha announced, her voice tinged with both relief and an edge of something darker – apprehension, perhaps, or foreboding.

Ingrid felt it too, the sense that the very earth was shifting beneath them, the tectonic plates of destiny realigning in anticipation of what was to come. Her mind raced back to the revelations they'd uncovered, the hidden threats, the lurking dangers that they were only now beginning to understand.

The car slowed as they entered the outskirts of the town, drawing closer to the centre. Agatha slammed on the brakes, jolting everyone forward as the Mini skidded to a stop on a side street. The sudden halt left Ingrid's stomach somewhere several feet behind her, and her ears rang from the abrupt silence as the engine ceased its growling.

"We're here," Agatha said quietly, her eyes locking onto Ingrid's. "Now, it's up to us to make sure we do what needs to be done."

Ingrid's only response was a silent nod.

CHAPTER 40
DELIA

I t was drawing late into the evening by the time they returned to Myrtlewood. Delia had, with some reluctance, agreed to pile into Agatha's car rather than take her own. Time was of the essence and clearly it made logical sense to take a vehicle enhanced by magic that could move much faster than ordinary ones. Delia quickly regretted her decision, though she was glad she hadn't eaten dinner. She was certain she would have lost it during the moments when the car seemed to become airborne.

As they finally pulled into Myrtlewood, the enormous ice dome looming over the village glistened under the rising moon.

The air outside was chilly, so at Agatha's request they stayed in the car to plot their next moves. After everything she'd been through in the past few hours, the desperate and dangerous attempt to rescue her friend and the shockingly vile revelation that her husband had been fooling her all these years, secretly manipulating her, plotting every move, her mind was in a rather dark place. But the sight of the glistening half-orb of ice was so magically transcendent, it lifted her spirits, taking her out of her dreadful circular thoughts of regret and betrayal and into some kind of childlike fairy tale.

Delia's heart soared at the sight of it, and no matter what the buffoon, Jerry, had done, she knew he no longer had any power over her.

The others stared at the dome too, in wonder, until Ingrid's words brought them all back down to earth. "Now that the invisibility magic has been broken, we're all vulnerable."

"I'm sorry," Delia said.

"Not much use in apologising now," Agatha grumbled.

Delia sighed. "I didn't mean to betray you. I just needed to get Kitty out safely."

"Of course, you did, love," replied Marjie. "We have to do what we must for those we care about, for those we love."

"I'm not complaining," said Kitty, "although I did have a hairdresser appointment this afternoon. It's been a thrilling day aside from being stuck in that boring chair staring at the curtains for so long."

Delia shook her head. "You always were a thrill-seeker."

Kitty beamed. "And now, look! There's magic in the world. Marvellous, isn't it, darling?"

Delia shook her head. "What am I going to do with you? I can't very well drag you into more danger."

Kitty pouted. "That's a pity. Although I've probably had enough for one day. Is there somewhere around here I can get a drink?"

"Now you're talking," said Agatha. "I believe Sherry from the pub has a mulled mead stand inside the dome. That's probably our best bet tonight. Most of the businesses will be closed or have their own stalls. Winter Solstice is a pretty big deal."

There were rather a lot of people milling about. "Are they all from Myrtlewood?" Delia asked.

"Not all of them," said Marjie. "Winter Solstice isn't a public festival like the summer one, but many magical people enjoy coming here. This time of year is special, festive Yuletide and all that."

"That's right. I need to get on and plan my family Christmas," said Delia. "Assuming Gilly is actually going to come."

"Don't give her the option not to," said Marjie. "Just ask her what she needs to make it work for her."

"Brilliant," said Delia. "You've solved one problem. What are we going to do about that stupid order and my stupid ex-husband? It's rather a lot to take in, isn't it?"

"I never thought he had it in him," said Kitty, sounding almost impressed by Jerry for the first time in their long acquaintance.

"I didn't think much of him before," said Delia. "So perhaps this only adds to his character, strangely enough. I just can't believe I was so stupid as to marry him."

"It was quite clever of him to orchestrate all of that," said

Kitty. "But in an extremely stupid way, of course," she added at Delia's glare, before changing the subject. "Now what's the plan?"

"The winter solstice ritual in Myrtlewood is powerful," Agatha explained. "All the seasonal ones are. But this is the time that's especially important for crones."

"That's right," said Ingrid. "From what I gathered in my research, if we can harness the energy of the ritual, and combine it with the power of the book, it says we will find the way to the Keystone – the way will be illuminated for us."

"And what's the bet the Order will be there, trying to stop us?" asked Delia.

"I'm about ninety-nine percent sure they will be," Ingrid admitted. "Unless they have some other secret agenda that we're not aware of. Which is entirely possible, given that they've been around for a long time, which leaves a lot of room for scheming and dastardly plans."

"That's right." Delia grimaced. "Jerry said that he was born into the Order. I guess we totally underestimated their horrendous cult and the lengths it will go to. It makes me question everything."

"Don't let him get to you, love," said Marjie, patting Delia on the shoulder. "I suspect the only reason he revealed all that to you is to undermine you tonight – to send you into a spiral. He's trying to destroy you and you are far too strong to be manipulated anymore, you hear me?"

Delia took a deep breath and nodded. "I think you're right.

He was expecting a very different reaction, not me and Kitty laughing at him. Perhaps a few weeks ago all this would have sent me into a psych ward or at least to bed with a hot water bottle and Valium for a few days, but despite all those years of manipulation, that man is nothing to me now. I'm angry, yes."

"And you deserve to be angry!" Kitty added.

"Of course I do," Delia said. "But I'm not letting him win. I'm not going to lose my head with rage or dive into despair. I'm the one in charge here, and I'm going to make the rage work for me, not the other way around."

"That's the spirit!" said Ingrid. "Now, let's get to it."

"But what am I going to do with Kitty?" Delia asked, glancing at her best friend. "Aside from getting you drunk on mulled mead, which might not actually be very sensible at a time like this."

"I don't know," said Kitty. "I'll give the mead a whirl as long as it's not too sweet."

"I've got friends who can look after you," said Marjie. "If you stay with them tonight, Kitty, the rest of us will work together and restore the Crone Magic."

Ingrid nodded. "Yes, then we can access our invisibility again. And we'll all be much better protected. This time we can extend it to our friends and family. We will have much more power once we have unleashed the next level of Crone magic; I'm sure of it."

"What am I signing up for?" Delia asked. "I'd never agree to a contract unless I've read the fine print. Gilly would scold me too much."

"None of us know exactly," said Agatha. "But there might not be a huge choice in the matter."

Delia surrendered to a new internal resolve. "I suppose if it's going to protect the people I care about and give me enough power to fight off my horrendous ex and his stupid order of red felted loons, I might not have much choice."

They quickly hashed out a plan, bearing in mind that they had very little information to go on, and then got out of the car to face a blast of chilly winter air.

CHAPTER 41
THE CLERIC

The Cleric emerged from the theatre, the air outside suddenly thick with tension, as if the universe itself had been a spectator to Father Benedict's shocking revelation. He felt the rough texture of the stone steps beneath his black shoes as he descended. The theatre's red velvet and gold décor that had once enveloped him in a sense of gravitas now felt like the ornamentations of a twisted farce. Even the balmy night air felt different – less pure, carrying an unfamiliar and uncomfortable weight.

His eyes landed on the nondescript black motor car waiting in the alleyway. He walked toward it, each step heavier than the last, his feet encased in shoes that felt like lead. The door opened with a mechanical click as he approached, and he silently slid into the back seat, next to Father Benedict.

The man he had once held in the highest esteem, a fellow

life-long servant to the Order. Now he had exposed himself as a monumental hypocrite.

He spent all those years with a WOMAN! And mistresses at that! The Cleric's skin crawled with revulsion at the very thought. He looked out the window, the passing cityscape blurring into an indistinct muddle of light and shadow, much like his feelings at that moment. The tainted scent of cologne, once comforting in its familiarity, now seemed to exacerbate his nausea.

As the engine hummed to life and the car started moving, he felt a vibration seep into his bones, each thrum a physical reminder of his internal disquiet. The city lights streamed by, blurring into streaks that seemed to mock his darkening thoughts. He stared out of the window but saw nothing, the external world rendered meaningless by his internal turmoil.

For years, he had listened in awe to tales of Father Benedict's noble sacrifices, of his pious struggles in the field, only to learn that the man had indulged in the most base of human frailties. The Cleric had always felt a kinship with him, born as they were into the Order, unlike the newcomers recruited from something called the Dark Web – a magic that the Cleric barely understood. Those incels, as they were called, lost souls lured in by the promise of purpose, ready to devote themselves to the Order and forget their old lives under the embrace of the Almighty...But the Cleric didn't need to be recruited, like Benedict, he was born for his role. Now, however, the Cleric wondered if any of it mattered. Was Father Benedict any different from those new recruits, when it came to the corruption of the soul?

The Cleric's gloved hands clenched into fists on his lap. The whole operation, every meticulous plan and scheme, now came under scrutiny. He had been part of kidnapping plots, silent coups, and intricate machinations, always secure in the righteousness of his cause.

How could a man soaked in sin truly lead such divine missions?

Each bump on the road jarred him, pulling him further from the sanctuary of his former beliefs. The entire foundation of his faith had been shaken, not just in the man sitting next to him but in the very Order that defined his existence.

Women were considered by the Order to be inferior, sinful, corrupting influences. The fact that Father Benedict, the man leading their most sacred mission, had been so deeply entangled with them was more than just shocking – it was revolting. The Cleric felt his stomach churn, his skin crawling as if he could physically shake off the disgust that now clung to him.

This revulsion was further magnified by the sudden realisation that Father Benedict had not been labouring in the field as he had imagined. There were no covert self-sacrificing operations, no life-risking reconnaissance, no sacred tasks. Instead, there had been a woman, a marriage, and a lifetime of sin paraded as sacrifice. This realisation was not just appalling, it was destabilising. It made the Cleric question not just the kidnapping plan they had so meticulously crafted, but the validity of their entire operation, of every operation they had ever conducted.

The grim streets of the city rolled past, each one an artery in a body of doubt and disillusionment. As he sat in the car, rigid, eyes staring but unseeing, the Cleric felt the weight of a profound, unsettling question settle over him: if Father Benedict, a lifelong servant of the Order, could fall so far, what did that mean for the rest of them? What did it mean for him?

The motorcar moved forward, despite it all, but in that moment, the Cleric was spiralling into an abyss, the walls lined with questions he had never thought he'd need to ask.

The air inside the car felt heavier, thickening with each passing moment, as if absorbing the weight of his disquiet.

The Cleric sat there, sharing the confined space with a man he could no longer trust or admire, lost in a labyrinth of doubt and disillusionment, questioning not just the mission, but his very place in the Order. The Order had been his structure. His purpose. His guiding discipline in life. The dark road stretched ahead, but for the first time, the Cleric felt completely and utterly lost.

CHAPTER 42
DELIA

Despite all the danger plaguing Delia's mind, she couldn't help but feel the thrill of excitement. There was festive magic in the air as people milled around, going from stall to stall outside the dome.

Inside, the most fabulous offerings were available.

She could no longer deny the deep desire of her heart to live in a world full of magic, not when faced with a marketplace of charmed gifts: snow globes came alive with miniature, animated landscapes; crystalised snowflake pendants, promising luck and purity; bells that, when rung, invited the blessings of warmth, safety, and abundance. Every item was infused with solstice magic, and many would make great gifts for the grandchildren. Delia felt a pang of longing. If only they could know about magic and enjoy all this!

She enjoyed a warming goblet of mulled mead with Kitty

while Marjie went to check on Rosemary and Athena, who seemed in good spirits, from across the room anyway. Delia waved to them, and they returned the gesture.

Delia felt a pang of longing, wishing that Gilly and the children could be here so that they could be part of this world and enjoy it with her.

Kitty was enthralled by it all, dragging Delia past all the stalls and pointing at everything, marvelling in delight. She led them back outside to the hot chocolate stand.

Marjie's good friend Papa Jack and his son were serving delicious beverages designed to invoke even more of a festive spirit than was already in the air.

"I don't suppose you've seen Marjie about?" Papa Jack asked. Delia smiled at him. "She's just in there with Rosemary," she said, unsure of what to say next. He blushed a little. "She's a good friend. I understand if she's busy. She told me there's trouble afoot."

"That's putting it lightly," said Kitty with an eyebrow raised.

Delia tried to not alarm anyone more than was necessary.

Delia could tell Papa Jack cared deeply for Marjie, but she also knew that her wonderful new friend was recovering from a rather devastating end to her long marriage and was busy nurturing and helping everyone else around her, probably as a coping mechanism.

Delia did wish Marjie would take some time to look after herself. She deserved happiness too, after all.

Papa Jack handed her a steaming cup and Delia took a long delicious sip.

The hot chocolate was just what Delia needed to lift her spirits. It was invigorating, making her tingle with joy and anticipation. "I think the play is about to start," said Papa Jack. "We might close up for the night."

Delia and Kitty wandered back into the elaborate ice dome. "This is just spectacular," said Kitty. "I love how it's magically bigger on the inside! Gosh, I wish I knew about this stuff when I was younger."

"You're telling me," said Delia. "I'm sure my grandmother did, but she died when I was so young. And my parents, well... they're not around to ask now, but I suppose it wasn't really their thing, if they ever knew about it in the first place."

"Well, it's never too late to have a second childhood," said Kitty, producing a bottle from her handbag.

"What's that?" Delia asked.

"I bought it from the market. Some kind of spirit, I think."

Delia snickered. "I hope you know what you're getting yourself into with that."

"We're about to find out," said Kitty with a grin. "Cheers to magic!"

The audience began to mill around the stage and some started to take their seats.

Marjie appeared with a warm smile, leading a beautiful woman who was probably in her thirties with long, dark brown hair over towards them. "This is Ursula," Marjie said.

Delia recognised her as the other sister from the Apothecary. She waved to Ashwyn as Marjie introduced her to Kitty as well.

"They have room for you to stay with them tonight, Kitty."

"I don't need a babysitter," said Kitty, slightly disgruntled.

"Not a babysitter," Marjie clarified. "It's just that we have something to do, as you well know. And you can't come with us. It's far too dangerous."

"I feel left out," Kitty protested. "But I suppose I'll be alright with this." She held up the purple bottle.

"Actually, Ursula has a lot of potions that you might be interested in," Marjie said.

"Tell me more," said Kitty, putting her arm around Ursula.

As her friend was busy, now absorbed in conversations about magical skincare products, Delia turned back to Marjie.

"Are Agatha and Ingrid casing the joint?" Delia asked.

Marjie nodded. "Yes, and we have a little time. First of all, there's going to be a play, and then the ritual. Oh look, the play is about to start," Marjie said.

Ferg, the rather pompous mayor, whom Delia had met a couple of times, made some announcements with grand hand gestures, and then a pantomime unfolded, which seemed to be loosely based on local mythology. Though the overwrought acting made Delia cringe.

"I know this is just a local play, but it is hard for me to watch," she admitted as the performance wrapped up and people began to mill around.

"Well, you know what they say. Don't criticise if you're not willing to help fix it," said Marjie with a cheeky grin.

"What does that mean?" asked Delia.

"Instead of complaining, do something about it," Marjie explained.

Delia chuckled. "You're suggesting I get into the local theatre scene? Ferg certainly wants me to."

"I don't see why not," Marjie said. "You've got the skills, and you've got the time now. Maybe you can find a new love for it."

Delia shrugged. "Maybe you're right." Though her tone was still rather uncertain.

Just then, Delia heard a barking sound and turned to see a little dog, the one she'd met several times before, with its gold and black back and white belly, trotting towards them.

"It's the beagle again," she said with a grin. "What do you want, little pup?" She bent down to give him pats. "I wonder who his owner is."

The puppy looked at her with sparkling deep brown eyes, yapping happily before rolling on his belly for more pats.

"I'd say he's yours," said Marjie.

"Mine? I don't have any pets. I haven't for years. Gilly had a bunny once, but that ended rather badly."

"No, not a pet," said Marjie. "I'd say he's your familiar."

"Familiar?"

Marjie smiled. "He keeps coming back to you, waiting to see if you've fully embraced your magic yet. I can tell he isn't connected to anyone else. He's hoping you'll accept him."

Delia looked into the big brown eyes that beseeched her for more pats. "You're joking! That's a real thing? We don't just have talking cats who are ancient cursed gods, here; we also have witches' familiars?"

"That's absolutely right," said Marjie. "And I'd say for sure that this one is yours. No one is quite certain how the magic of familiars works. I've never had one myself, but some say it is the power of a witch's magic that draws a special animal. I believe it's more personal than that – some animal souls have special connections with human beings and they come into the world to seek us out and take care of us."

Delia giggled like a three-year-old. She felt as if it was Christmas morning, and she was opening a box to find a puppy.

She'd always wanted one as a child, but her parents never relented. And as an adult she never had the chance. Jerry was allergic to cats and dogs. So even in her later years, when her life was settled enough to have one, she'd never risked it.

She felt the bond running through her to the adorable, yet obviously intelligent, animal.

"What's your name, pup?" she asked, looking into his beautiful eyes. A word popped into her head. "Torin?"

The beagle have a happy yap and turned around in a circle.

"A perfect name!" Marjie declared. "It means chief, I think. And this little boy is a chiefly presence for sure."

Delia beamed at her and patted the dog some more.

Just then, the mayor and someone who was apparently a

druid announced that the winter solstice ritual was about to start.

"You stand in the direction of South for fire," said Marjie. "I'll be in the West for water, Ingrid in the North for earth, and Agatha in the East for air. That's where our elements will be strongest."

"And what do I do during the ritual?" Delia asked.

"Try not to do too much, actually," Marjie muttered as the market stalls around them vanished and so did the chairs, as the room became rather empty besides all the people who were quickly forming into a large circle. "Try to just receive the energy. Winter is the time for reflection. Quiet time to really harness the energy you need. Trying to do too much will only get in the way. We just need to be open to it."

Delia nodded and followed Marjie's instructions towards the south of the circle. The little dog followed her and sat down next to her feet as she took her place.

As the ritual began, she found herself standing right next to the person summoning the element of fire in the south. As they did so, she felt a burning sensation.

She glanced down, relieved to find her clothes were still intact and nothing was actually alight. She then connected again with that feeling, that passion, that drive, the spark, the inspiration and initiation, the rebirth that was all part of the energy of fire.

It was invigorating.

As the ritual progressed, she felt the other elements as they were called; Delia sensed their energies but in a more minor way. The whole ritual seemed eerily familiar to her, though she'd never participated in anything quite like it.

As the wintery chant rang out around the room, Delia allowed herself to open up to the energy of winter, just as Marjie had instructed. It was the time when the seeds lay dormant in the ground, waiting to burst forth; the trees stood still and bare while animals found shelter and hibernated. The time when the fires traditionally burned long into the night. And the earth rested and restored itself, ready for a new cycle to begin.

There was something ancient and primal about this time, as if she was connecting with her ancestors who had walked this land for centuries, for millennia. Were some of them Crones too? Were more of them witches, not just Etty, but further back in history? Were they persecuted by zealots like the Order? Were they tortured for their beliefs, for their power, even though they were just trying to heal and help, to enjoy their lives as best they could?

She felt a stabbing pain and agony burning through her, for all this suffering, followed by a deep ancient rage.

Rage can be destructive, but it also inspires action.

She could harness her own rage. She could use it to do good, not just to accidentally set things on fire, or burn herself out.

CHAPTER 43
THE SHEPHERD

The scent of damp earth and smouldering fires filled his nostrils as Father Benedict left the stale air of the motorcar behind and made his way toward the large, antiquated tent that stood as the nerve centre of his operations. The Cleric, who had been riding beside him, was oddly silent during the entire journey, adding a layer of tension that Father Benedict found both distracting and mildly annoying.

He had expected praise and awe from his underling, but perhaps the younger man was simply jealous and fighting with his own arrogance in the face of the humility demanded by the Almighty.

The large tent loomed ahead, its canvas walls glowing softly in the ambient light of lanterns. He pushed past the flap, entering into the warm, musty air within. It smelled of mildew, ink, and sweat – the scent of duty, struggle, and holy work.

Guards clad in the Order's traditional attire moved about in coordinated chaos, their scurrying movements reminiscent of ants at a feast.

He walked purposefully towards his operations table, which was strewn with maps, arcane texts, and various magical implements in a way that was unreasonably out of order, but that did not matter when he was riding high on his latest victory.

His eyes narrowed, images of Delia Spark flashing through his mind like a flickering candle. Ah, Delia, his unwilling muse in a grander design than she could ever fathom. Her face had not been as distraught as he'd imagined. She'd laughed at him, defied him, and this only stoked the fire of his determination.

Father Benedict had meticulously orchestrated every aspect of this divine mission, right down to the last incantation. Delia was the weakest link in the ancient puzzle that was the magic of the Elemental Crones of Myrtlewood. She was unaware of magic, unlike the others. She was an easy target, ripe for manipulation, and he'd taken up the challenge with utmost precision and determination – decades of painstaking work and sacrifice that only the Almighty could truly understand had led to that moment.

He felt a shiver of pride crawl up his spine, stimulating him.

"Jameson, move our agents into position around the forest!" he barked at a young disciple poring over a stack of parchment. "And make sure the men are armed!"

"As you command, Father," the disciple replied, scrambling to carry out his orders.

Father Benedict turned to another underling. "Martin, see that the ceremonial blades are properly sanctified and ready!"

"Immediately, Father," he responded, hurrying off.

But even as he issued commands, a stubborn knot of doubt lodged itself in his mind. The audacity of those wretched women! They had laughed in the face of his holy mission. He'd deceived Delia for years, all as part of his elaborate ruse. She had known him as the charming, caring, and amiable 'Jerry', who had swooped in and rescued her from her greatest failure, who had stood by her and supported her lovingly for so many years. Now, knowing that it had all been a set-up, she should have been crushed, but if she was, she'd hidden it well. The divorce was the first shock. That was designed to unsettle her and finally send her off into the magical world.

The Order had curated the whole scenario with him, the Crimson Shepard, as the lead choreographer.

He'd willingly held her back from magic for many years, so that she didn't learn too much too soon. At the ripe old age of sixty-three she was a mere novice and not at all prepared to be an Elemental Crone, yet she could fulfil that one part of unleashing the buried magic.

Tonight's revelation should have destroyed her. She should have been broken, emotionally shattered.

But the Delia he had confronted earlier was not the Delia he remembered.

She had always been unnervingly strong – a vile attribute passed down from her magical ancestors, no doubt. Yet now, she had looked almost radiant, shining with a defiant light that troubled him.

She had laughed at his revelation. The woman's gall had taken him aback. Delia had always been unpredictably tenacious, but her reaction this time had been entirely unanticipated. He clenched his fists, quelling the frustration that threatened to boil over. No matter. She wouldn't be a concern for much longer.

Father Benedict stood back and surveyed the chaos around him. It would have to do.

"Ready the beast!" he commanded, his voice echoing throughout the tent. His underlings halted, staring at him for a brief moment before springing into action, setting in motion the next phase of his immaculate plan.

Yes, he'd certainly have the last laugh. Once the Order seized the Crones' powers, once they unlocked that potent magic from its ancient sanctuaries, then would come the Almighty's promised reckoning.

Father Benedict stood over his operations table, well aware that the universe itself was aligning in his favour. Delia Spark had fallen right into his trap, and oh, how he would relish in her downfall.

CHAPTER 44
DELIA

As the winter solstice ritual came to an end, people began to disperse before the crones gathered in the north of the circle. That was when it happened.

Delia felt, at first, a stab of intuition, and then she heard barking. The beagle puppy ran towards one of the entrances and began growling and making a racket.

"Torin!" Delia called after him.

The Crones turned to see a group of Order members in red robes barring the nearest exit – just where they were planning to go through a moment later.

"We should go the other way," Marjie whispered.

"No," said Delia. "We're not going to let them stand in our way, we're not going to cower."

"What do you suggest then?" Agatha asked with a knowing smirk.

Delia raised an eyebrow. "I bet those robes are flammable."

Everyone else was outside of the radius of danger. It was just the Order members, surrounded by an icy gateway.

She closed her eyes, connecting with that ancestral rage again, sending a burst of it out towards the guards standing in their way.

There were shrieks and cries from the crowd as flames erupted and the red-hooded men dispersed, rolling on the ground, trying to extinguish the fire.

The crones walked slowly and confidently through the exit, ignoring the outraged cries of their enemies.

Delia tried to pretend that she wasn't enjoying all this rather too much. She was reminded of a '90s movie that Gillian was once infatuated with called *The Craft*, except instead of being teenagers walking through school in dishevelled uniforms, they were powerful crones walking side by side out into the moonlight on winter solstice.

"Hopefully that'll teach them to leave us alone," said Marjie.

"Somehow I doubt it," said Delia, casting a glance back towards the dome.

"I'm so proud of you, dear," said Marjie. "That was brilliant. You've really got mastery of your power."

"For now, anyway," said Delia, feeling rather pleased with herself.

The puppy barked happily, following them out.

"Sit," Delia instructed. The small dog did as he was told.

"Now, stay here, Torin," she implored him. "Coming with us is too dangerous."

The beagle whimpered a little and Delia gave him a good pat, extending her gratitude for his assistance. "Thank you for your help." She scratched behind his ears. "However, I need you to remain here now. It's not safe."

The little dog pawed at the floor a few times before whining. Delia leaned down to its level, meeting its gaze. "Look, if you're as smart as I think you are, then I need to keep you safe just as much as you need to keep me safe. Okay?"

The beagle returned her gaze with those big, innocent, puppy-dog eyes.

Delia sighed. "Alright, if you need a job, go find Kitty. Make sure she's safe. Okay? Let no harm come to her. She's new to all of this. You understand, don't you?"

In response, the dog gave what sounded like an affirmative grunt. His tail wagged energetically as he circled around a few times before returning to Delia. He sought a few more pats and ear scratches before trotting off.

"Stay with the nice people," Delia called after him. "And stay away from anyone in a red cloak."

Ingrid's voice sounded from behind her. "Have you quite finished there? We've put up some temporary cloaking and magical barriers. We only have a few minutes at most before the Order breaks through. Time is of the essence."

"Yes," Delia replied, turning towards her. "Let's go."

"Now," said Ingrid, "down to business. We must combine our powers and bring forth that energy of the Winter Solstice, connecting with the waning moon, so that the ancient magic shows us the way. If it helps you to concentrate, perhaps we could just speak slowly, saying our element over and over again."

They began to chant, Delia saying the word 'fire'. She could recognise the others in their distinct voices, Marjie with her nurturing tones of 'water', Agatha's scratchy voice of 'air', and Ingrid sternly saying 'earth'.

Altogether, the sound was ancient and beautiful. Something stirred in Delia. She felt a lightness and looked down to see that her torso was indeed glowing, shining a beam that reached out into the centre of the group, joining together with the emanating forces from the other Crones.

Ingrid raised her arms. "Powers of the Ancient Ones, powers of the Old Ones. We are here, the four Myrtlewood Crones, chosen by our heritage and by the elements themselves. Guide us to where we might unlock the timeless magic protecting all that is good; protecting our town and our world against those who seek to extinguish us and destroy the balance of the world. We are here to restore it. We are here to pledge ourselves..."

"Stop babbling," said Agatha. "Look!"

The light of their powers between them began to glow, combined with the light of the low crescent moon. It condensed into a star and began to move outwards.

"Do we follow it?" said Marjie.

"Wait." Ingrid held her back.

The light grew and opened up into a doorway, a kind of portal.

"I think we go through," said Agatha.

"Of course we go through," said Ingrid. "Didn't do all this for nothing."

"You first, Agatha," said Marjie.

"Why me?"

"Start with the East and the element of Air," Ingrid explained.

"Oh fine!" Agatha huffed and took a step through the portal, disappearing into thin air.

Ingrid went next with no fanfare. Then, it was Delia's turn. She held her breath, then stepped through.

She expected the portal to change her somehow, call to her, transform her, but she felt almost exactly the same as she stepped into different terrain.

The ground beneath her feet squelched.

"What on earth is this?" she asked.

"We are in a swamp," said Agatha.

"A sacred swamp," said Marjie, bringing up the rear as the portal closed behind them.

"A swamp's a swamp," Agatha grunted. "And I'm getting my new boots all mucky."

Delia giggled.

"If that's the worst thing you've faced, then you're lucky," said Ingrid. "Not a fan of mud?"

"Who is?" Agatha grumbled.

"Well, it is fitting for crones, isn't it?" said Marjie.

Agatha glared at her. "You would say that."

"I'm serious," Marjie added. "The swamp...emotionally and metaphorically, represents darkness, stillness, the void. That's where our magic comes from."

"I didn't come all this way to be a swamp creature," Agatha muttered.

"Quit your whining," said Ingrid. "Look."

Small lights dotted the ground in front of them, illuminating a path through the swamp which was only slightly less muddy than just walking directly into the puddles.

"We've come this far," said Delia. "Let's get a move on. At least the Order aren't out here. I'm sure they wouldn't want to soil their robes. Jerry always hated getting dirty."

"And you married him, dear," said Marjie with a chuckle.

They made their way through the muck, guided by the lights. The darkness was murky, thick with mist that hung in the air, seeming more magical than regular fog.

They trudged on deeper into the swamp.

"Do you think this is where you thought it was on the map?" Delia asked.

"Well, I certainly hope so," said Ingrid. "I don't like being wrong. And if it is where I thought it was, it means we've taken a shortcut. We don't have to trek all the way through the forest."

"Portals are very convenient," Delia agreed.

Up ahead, she could see something, a structure of some kind.

Not quite tall enough to be a building, but it stood out against the low lying swampy surroundings enough that it had to be deliberately placed there.

"There it is," said Ingrid, pointing. "The Crone stone."

"Crone stone?" Delia asked. "That's what you wrote on the map, was it?"

"Of course, couldn't you read it?"

Delia shrugged. Now wasn't the time to offend the sternest witch she knew.

Before they could reach the stone, Delia smacked right into something hard in the air in front of her. They were halted by an invisible barrier.

"What on earth?" she said.

"Do you think it's the Order?" asked Marjie, her hand tapping against the air, making a sound like glass.

"It's a magical shield," said Agatha. "It's protecting the stone."

"It must be riddle," Agatha muttered. "Maybe there's a magic word."

"Surely we should be able to get through. We are the Crones, right?" said Marjie. "I mean, the magic worked for us. It led us here."

Ingrid peered sternly at the invisible barrier. "It's some kind of test."

While Agatha and Marjie tried different charms against the shield, and Ingrid supervised, Delia experienced a creeping sensation running down her spine.

She looked around her into the darkness. Could it be that the shield was set up by the Order? Was it another trap? Something about the whole scenario was eerie.

The Order had been around for hundreds, maybe thousands, of years. They'd orchestrated so much, including her own sham of a marriage. And while some of their manoeuvrings were clumsy, and there was certainly plenty of room for human error, if they'd gone to such great lengths, it seemed strange that they were absent now.

Delia had been some kind of pawn her whole life without even knowing it. Jerry had humiliated her secretly; he'd wooed her in her weakest moment, ensured that she was captivated by the magic of the theatre rather than discovering her own true heritage.

Every step had been calculated.

And while the marriage was over now, surely the divorce was just as much a part of his plan. Had he been sending her to Myrtlewood at the right time?

Anyone could be in league with him, even perhaps one of the other Crones. She eyed Agatha suspiciously, though it seemed doubtful that someone so incredibly stroppy would get in line for a bunch of musty monks.

Still, Delia felt as if she was missing something.

Surely if the Order had had thousands of years to study the Crones, they would know about this place, especially as this was not the first time Crone magic had been rekindled. Ingrid and

Marjie seemed to think it happened every hundred years or so, along with a rising threat.

Was the Order the rising threat? Or was it something else? Her thoughts strayed to that darkness that had haunted her visions, to the nightmares that she'd had all her life, and to the mythical beasts, terrible and more bloodthirsty than any lawyer.

CHAPTER 45
MARJIE

The swamp's thick, humid air clung to Marjie's skin as the night sounds resonated around her – the distant croaks of frogs, and the hum of unseen insects amid the occasional hoot of an owl. The low crescent moon cast a subtle silvery light over the water, making the surface glimmer.

The environment was thick with magical energy. She could almost feel the vibrations tingling on her fingertips. But no matter what charms they tried, the shield wouldn't budge, and none of Agatha's analysis was doing them any good.

"You're thinking about this too logically," Marjie said.

"Oh, yes," Agatha quipped with her signature sarcasm. "And what would you have me do, oh wise one?"

"You're the rational one, aren't you?" Marjie retorted, her intuition buzzing within her, a familiar warmth in her gut. "Air and all that. It relates to the logical mind."

"Yes, so I should know what I'm talking about," Agatha shot back.

"Or perhaps you need to let go a bit," Marjie said, her tone gentle, sensing the weight of the Crone Stone's magic pressing upon them all.

"What are you implying?" Ingrid interjected, her voice stern, as if she was chastising a group of unruly children.

Marjie put her hands on her hips, feeling a rush of energy. "Well, to be Crones, we have to go through intuitive processes, not just the logical ones. Sometimes emotion is the antidote to reason. So I'm going to ask Agatha, what is it that she least wants to do right now?"

"Fall into the mud, I suppose," Agatha grumbled.

Marjie's heart leaped. "Aha! That's perfect."

She could almost feel the pulse of the swamp, guiding her.

"Are you serious?" Delia asked, her voice a mix of incredulity and amusement. "That's absurd. My shoes are already mucky enough."

Agatha gave Delia a conspiratorial look. "Finally you speak some sense."

Marjie's patience wore thin. "Look, all the charms you've tried haven't worked, Agatha. All your rational magic, and all your knowledge that comes from books, are not going to be any good to us here."

Agatha raised an eyebrow. "If you're so sure, *you* go first."

Marjie paused, feeling the swamp's energy seep into her. Then, brimming with determination, she carefully placed her handbag on the path. She unravelled her scarf from her neck, letting the chill of the evening seep through her skin. She peeled off her shoes and soon the cold, squishy mud tickled her toes with a squelch as she stepped barefoot into the swamp.

Delia's gasp echoed in the night as Marjie's feet squished into the soft, wet dirt, but Marjie was undeterred.

"Is that it?" Agatha sneered. "What are you trying to prove, you moonstruck mandrake?"

"This," Marjie declared, lowering herself down till she was almost in a sitting position. She felt the cool, grainy texture of the mud, feeling its embrace. The very act of getting muddy seemed to amplify her connection to her own magic.

The uneven surface of the stones caressed her palms, contrasting sharply with the warmth of her skin. She began to edge her way towards the inviting mud puddle, anticipating the sensations that awaited her.

Delia covered her mouth with her hand, her fingers brushing against her lips. "It's painful to watch."

Marjie's heart raced, every sense heightened by her defiant act. "Sometimes life is full of crap you'd rather avoid," she declared, feeling the slimy mud seeping between her fingers.

"It doesn't mean you have to immerse yourself in it," Ingrid scolded, her voice layered with maternal concern.

"I disagree," said Marjie. "You've just got to wade through it."

"Really, Marjoram. This is no time to behave like a blooming toadstool!"

"Maybe it's the perfect time!" Marjie's laughter bubbled up from her chest, the sensation of the mud embracing her body feeling oddly comforting. "Oh! Oh my goodness. You know, it's funny. I don't even feel cold. It's like the mud is whispering ancient secrets to me."

"Someone's had too much mulled mead," Agatha muttered sarcastically, her nose upturned in disgust. "And it's not me this time."

"I feel as though I need a shower just watching." Delia shivered, her eyes never leaving the muddy spectacle.

"You'll see," Marjie replied. "But I am going to need someone to help me up, though."

"Oh, very well," said Agatha, her words dripping with resignation.

But as she moved closer, she lost her footing, and the mud swallowed her, transforming her once pristine appearance. Marjie's chuckle resonated through the air, full of pure amusement, as if she'd just witnessed a potion gone hilariously wrong.

"Maybe it's too much of a risk to ask anyone else to help me out now." Marjie smirked, sensing the thick consistency of the mud around her. "But I am going to give this a try." Her determination evident as she began her muddy journey.

"Now, I'd rather have thought that I'd be far too old for this," Marjie mused aloud, feeling each movement and tug of the mud around her limbs. "The mud seems to be invigorating me!" she exclaimed, every cell of her body coming alive with glee.

CHAPTER 46
DELIA

Delia gritted her teeth. She wanted to help Marjie as she crawled along the ground towards the barrier, but didn't know how to do that.

Agatha continued to grumble from where she sat in the mud and Ingrid looked on sternly. "You're all behaving like children," she said.

"Come on, Marjie. I'll give you a hand," said Delia.

"I'm almost there!" said Marjie.

"It's not going to work," Agatha muttered.

Just then, a bright light shot out from the Keystone.

Delia stared into it trying to make out what had happened and quickly deduced that Marjie had come in contact with the barrier and it was now responding to her muddy form.

It shimmered and opened.

"See! Ahaha!" Marjie crowed in triumph as she hoisted

herself on the other side of the shield.

"Brilliant," said Ingrid, and strode forward, but the barrier repelled her.

She stood back again, rubbing her head. "Oh, bother!"

Agatha laughed. "I guess we're all gonna have to get in the mud."

"I thought that was your worst nightmare," said Delia.

"It's not so bad once you're in here," Agatha admitted.

Ingrid took a tentative step forward and then slipped ungracefully into a puddle.

"Ugh!" said Ingrid, wiping splatters of mud from her cheeks.

"What are you complaining about?" said Agatha. "You're the earth witch!"

"Not the mud witch," Ingrid insisted. "I'm not afraid of a little dirt, but that doesn't mean I'm keen on getting filthy and sodden. Let's get on with it!"

The two grumpy crones sat side by side and looked at Delia expectantly.

Delia shrugged. She took off her jacket and cast her bag aside carefully on a rock. Then, wincing a little, she removed her boots and socks. Her bare feet squelched into the mud. She made the kind of noise a child makes when trying to get into the ocean on a freezing cold day.

"We haven't got all night," said Agatha, gleefully smearing mud onto her arms.

"Getting into the spirit of things, I see," said Delia.

She thought it might be safer to follow Marjie's lead and

crawl, but before she could get there, her feet slipped on a slippery rock. She hurtled to the ground, expecting pain. Instead she froze.

"What the..."

Delia's head hovered inches above the ground, clearly stopped by a charm, while a hand caught her arm to support her.

"Thanks, whoever that was."

"Don't mention it," said Ingrid.

Delia smiled and laughed. Rolling around in the mud! The whole situation was ridiculous, but Marjie was right. The more she embraced the swamp, the more powerful and strangely warm she felt despite the chilly evening.

"There's something about this that makes me feel so alive!" said Delia.

"It's not bad, is it?" Ingrid admitted.

"I thought Marjie was mad, but it turns out water is the intuitive element," said Agatha. "And even a cracked cauldron can store potatoes."

"Well, this clock is ready to activate some Crone powers," Marjie called. "Get over here, you lot!"

Delia couldn't help rolling around in the mud just a little bit more before making a somewhat slippery journey over towards Marjie.

Ingrid had gotten there first, entering the barrier with no trouble at all now that she was suitably muddied. And Agatha was close behind her.

Delia looked around one last time as she approached, her feet slipping slightly on the rocks of the path.

She couldn't help feeling as though she was being watched. If the Order had come all the way out here, why hadn't they stopped them?

"I wonder if this is such a good idea," Delia said.

"Don't dilly-dally," said Agatha. "Get your fiery butt in here."

Delia sighed. "Fine."

She took another tentative step towards the barrier, and it opened before her, swallowing her up. The air inside was comfortably warm and pleasant, and despite the mud caking her body now, she felt oddly clean – perhaps in an emotional way rather than a physical one.

"We all take our places," said Ingrid as she studied the enormous stone in front of them.

The structure was circular, with an elevated stone in the centre and another one surrounding it, lower to the ground with room enough for all the crones to stand around it. Delia noticed patterns etched in the stone, barely visible in the low light. They looked to be something like runes or sigils that she could not understand in the slightest.

"That's the symbol for fire," said Marjie, pointing to a triangle.

"Thanks." Delia moved towards that side of the stone.

"What do we do now?" Agatha asked once they'd taken their places.

"Well, you're supposed to be the clever one," said Marjie.

"I'm just a stopped clock, remember?" She chortled.

"Can you read the sigils?" Delia asked.

"Of course I can," said Agatha. "I just don't know about the context. These are very ancient symbols; they have different uses and meanings throughout time. I'd have to date them."

"We haven't got all day," said Marjie. "So what then?"

Ingrid frowned in concentration. "I suspect it goes a little bit like what we did earlier on to find this place. We all combine our powers. We connect with the stone and the ancient energy of the crones and the Winter Solstice."

"Wait a minute," said Delia. "What if the Order wants us to do this? I keep thinking about it."

"Don't be ridiculous. Why would they want us to be more powerful?" Agatha asked.

"Maybe they want to steal our power or something," Delia said. "Just think about it. It keeps coming back to me about how much my life was orchestrated by them. Would they really go to so much effort, only to totally drop the ball at the last minute? What if they've led us here, piece by piece, luring us towards this particular scenario? What if they knew we would come here right now?"

"I've thought along the same lines," said Ingrid. "But it changes nothing."

Delia looked around. She was sure she could see movement in the shadows of the swamp, but there was nothing clear or definitive.

"They can't get to us in here, dear," said Marjie. "We could barely get in here – not until we were caked in mud. And I don't think it'll work for them, since they're certainly not the Crones of Myrtlewood."

"That's a fair point," said Delia. "I just think we should have a plan, you know, be prepared for all eventualities. What will we do once we have power? What if it doesn't go the way we thought it would? What if it's hard to master and backfires on us?"

"Now you're sounding a bit like air," said Agatha. "I'm the one who overthinks things. I've already been through all of those scenarios and discounted most of them. Let me tell you, it will do you no good to think any more about them."

"Okay. If you're such a strategist, what do you think the plan should be?" Delia asked.

"We do what we can," Agatha replied. "We unlock the powers, and then we go after the Order, regardless of whether they've tracked us down already, or we have to hunt them to the ends of Britain and beyond...We put ourselves in the leader's seat."

"That's all very well and good," said Delia, "but what if they *already* have the upper hand?"

"Then we take the upper hand from them and slap them in the face with it," said Ingrid.

Delia laughed. "That's a plan I can get behind."

She still couldn't help looking over her shoulder. They might seem to be in the middle of nowhere, but she was sure somebody else was out there, watching and waiting.

CHAPTER 47
THE ROGUE

E merging from the portal, Declan felt the visceral grip of his own magic release him onto the sodden, squelching ground of a territory foreign to his senses. The swamp seemed alive, like a voracious entity. It seemed to swallow up everything around it.

The air was thick with a musky aroma, a blend of decaying leaves, stagnant water, and the earthy undertones of the swamp.

His pulse quickened, not from the oppressive aura of the swamp, nor from the looming shadows of his burden. It was her. Delia Spark. The enigma that persistently lingered in the recesses of his mind. An involuntary curse escaped his lips. He should be anywhere else but here.

He'd done his job for the night. He'd given the Order their precious information. He should be miles away, and he would be, but for the cursed magnetic pull that ensnared him, leading him deeper into murky peril.

The Cleric had merely nodded in satisfaction as Declan performed the seeking spell and revealed the location of the Crones – no longer protected by their powerful invisibility magic.

Clearly, that was her doing as well. That stubborn woman had stormed right into their trap totally aware of what she was doing. Declan wasn't aware of the details. He'd left London, hoping the call from the Order wouldn't come, hoping for peace and solitude. A few short hours later, he was summoned to a camp, and there amid the mildewed canvas structures, he'd carried out his contract, dutifully, despite his own resentment burning a hole in his chest.

He was a mere pawn in their game, just as the Crones were. Delia might be fiery and powerful and infuriatingly unpredictable, but the Order had centuries of plotting and a small army on their side.

Declan was yet to gather enough intel to understand exactly what the Order wanted, but whatever it was, his renewed burden of morality protested against it. He wished for the peace of earlier days when he'd had the freedom not to care as his eyes cased the swamp, seeking out the Crones.

Through the mist he spotted them. Four silhouettes of women, melding with the swamp as they cackled. Among them, Delia's laughter echoed, drawing him in.

The whole scene was surreal. The Myrtlewood Crones,

ageless and potent, almost seemed to dance with uncanny abandon.

The Order's malignant aura loomed, its intent palpable in the charged atmosphere.

Drawing back, Declan sought refuge behind an ancient willow, its bark cool and textured against his hand. Every sinew in his body yearned to shout a warning, to disrupt their revelry. But his contract forbade him from interfering, yet again.

It would be wise to leave now, to get as far away from here as he possibly could and avoid witnessing the battle ahead, power-less to intervene lest he lose everything.

Yet, he stood, transfixed. The juxtaposition struck him sharply. Here, on the brink of impending chaos, the Crones revelled in the sheer essence of their magic, their unity, their defiance. Their cackles cut through the tension in the air, as if laughter were an antidote to the power of corruption, and perhaps it was.

Declan's contemplation was jolted by a subtle movement in his periphery. Another figure, moving with deliberate stealth, advanced towards the swamp. An emissary of the Order, he surmised.

The end was nigh.

CHAPTER 48
DELIA

"Join hands," Ingrid instructed.

The four Crones reached out to clasp each other's fingers and palms.

There was something familiar about this, and not just from the recent days. Perhaps it was a resonance, not from this lifetime but another but from past lives. Did they exist along with all this other magic? Or could these be ancestral memories from Crones that came before her? Either way, standing there with the three sister Crones was like slipping into an old pair of comfortable leather boots or creaming the butter and sugar in a favourite family recipe in a well-used mixing bowl.

It felt good, comfortable, and right.

But then Ingrid began to speak in a haunting, deep voice, her eyes rolling back. "By the power of the old ones, we, the new Elemental Crones of Myrtlewood, beseech you..."

Delia felt her terror rising. The old ones – who were they? She was reminded of the terrifying force she'd seen in the darkness of the void.

What kind of primal monster was awakening within her? She tried to pull her hand away, but the grips of the other Crones were too tight as Ingrid continued to chant.

By the powers of the spirits of the ancient goddesses, Cerridwen, the Morrigan, Hecate, the Cailleach – the ancient goddesses whose power we revere and who bestow on us their great blessings. We unite to claim back what is rightfully ours.

"Is it too late to stop this?" Delia whispered to Marjie before turning her head out towards the swamp around them. She could have sworn she saw a figure in the darkness, not an enemy, but an ally, though surely it would be too dark to see anyone at all, at this point in the night.

"We can't stop now, dear," said Marjie. "Just be brave. Fear is in all of us, you know."

Perhaps Marjie was too intuitive for her own good. Delia would have grumbled about it, but instead of interrupting further, she turned inward.

Of course it was her own fear, yet again, getting in her way. Just like the fear of embarrassment and shame that had thrown her from the stage and the limelight, into Jerry's arms, forcing her to pour all her passion and drive into backstage rehearsals and to merely receive bouquets at the end of each production. Fears had controlled her then. And now she had additional ones related to magic and mythical beasts, not to mention fears that she was a mere pawn – after all, Jerry had manipulated for years without Delia even being aware of the level of his deceit.

Fear in itself wasn't a bad thing – was it? Delia reasoned that fear could protect a woman, a witch, anyone from a dangerous situation. But she knew from working with terrified actors over the years how primal fears could be; how the fear of embarrassment was actually the fear of survival.

Human beings evolved in small, nomadic groups in often harsh terrains, needing instinctively to stick together in the wild. Being rejected by the tribe meant certain death. Therefore, that fear that Delia had faced in her career was the fear of annihilation, just like it was right now.

Although, instead of embarrassment and shame haunting her in this moment, it was a real fear for her survival. Could she really trust these women she'd known for barely a fortnight, who didn't seemed to know what they were doing most of the time?

"We beseech you, old ones!" cried Ingrid, raising her hands as the others followed, their arms linked and rising towards the sky.

The earth trembled beneath them, and that's when Delia noticed definitive movement around the outside of their circle.

The Order was there, and they weren't even bothering to

hide anymore. Rows and rows of burgundy-clad guards or monks or soldiers, or whatever they were, surrounded them, illuminated by the glow of fiery torches.

"They're here," Delia whispered to Marjie, who peeked open her eyes. "We're surrounded by the Order. They knew we were going to be here all along. They—they ambushed us, just like I thought."

"They want to steal our power," said Agatha, grinning.

"What is there to smile about?" Delia asked.

Agatha pierced her with a look of steely determination. "I'd like to see them try."

CHAPTER 49
THE SHEPERD

F ather Benedict stood atop a raised hillock, the cool, damp ground beneath his leather boots giving him a vantage point over the sprawling swamp below. Despite the murkiness of the environment, his sharp eyes took in every detail, from the iridescent sheen of the wetland plants to the soft, otherworldly glow of the moonlight that illuminated the area. The air was thick with chilly humidity, causing his robes to cling uncomfortably to his skin. However, discomfort was the least of his concerns.

As he glanced around at the stagnant waters, the scent of decaying vegetation, mixed with the tang of mud, permeated the air, lending a heaviness to each breath he took. But beneath these sensory distractions, another smell lingered – the metallic scent of anticipation, of his soldiers ready for battle.

"Prepare the lines!" he commanded, his voice carrying

clearly through the dense fog. Soldiers of the Order of Crimson, dressed in their maroon uniforms, began to move with disciplined precision.

Spearmen formed the front line, their sharp-tipped weapons gleaming dully in the dim light. Behind them, archers nocked their arrows, the taut strings of their longbows waiting to be released.

Mages, dressed in dark cloaks, gathered in clusters, their fingers moving rhythmically as they prepared their incantations of protective spells and offensive incendiaries.

The Cleric, his most loyal disciple, approached him, a leather-bound scroll in hand and a steely look in his eyes. "Our scouts report that the Crones are gathered near the Stone, just as the tracker told us. Our intelligence suggests they aren't expecting an immediate assault."

Father Benedict nodded. "And the terrain?"

The Cleric unfurled the scroll, revealing a map of the swamp. "The ground is treacherous, Shepherd. But we've identified a few solid pathways that our troops can use to approach without getting mired. However, these routes are narrow, making them vulnerable to ambush."

Father Benedict's fingers traced the routes, his mind working rapidly. "We'll split our forces. Two detachments will take the flanks, drawing the Crones' attention. The main force will advance through the centre. And the mages?"

The Cleric looked up, his eyes grim. "Ready, but there's a

limit to how much magic they can wield in this environment. The swamp itself seems to resist our powers."

A smirk tugged at the corners of Father Benedict's lips. "Then we'll rely on good old steel and strategy, and our secret weapon of course. Signal the advance."

Torches were lit, casting eerie shadows on the water's surface as the soldiers began their march. The soft squelch of boots on wet ground and the muffled clang of armour filled the air. As they moved, Father Benedict could feel the tension rise, the weight of impending conflict pressing down on them all. But for the most part, the swamp was deceptively calm.

Suddenly, a bright flare shot up into the night sky from the direction of the Crone Stone. It burst into a myriad of colours, illuminating the swamp like daylight for a brief moment.

"They know we're here," the Cleric whispered.

"Good," Father Benedict responded coldly. "Let them see our might."

As the main force approached the Crone Stone, they could hear the soft murmur of voices, the Crones chanting in unison. The mages began their counter-spells, trying to disrupt the Crones' magic, while the spearmen formed a shield wall, ready to defend against any frontal assault.

The minutes dragged on, each one more tense than the last. Finally, Father Benedict gave the signal. From the shadows, a massive cage was wheeled forward. Inside, the beast known as the Beithíoch paced restlessly, its powerful form barely contained by the iron bars. Its mottled white fur tangled and dirty. Its eyes glowed with an inner fire, and its growls sent shivers down the spines of even the bravest soldiers.

With a nod from Father Benedict, the cage door was slowly opened. The Beithíoch paused for a moment, then with a mighty roar, it lumbered forward, heading straight for the Crones.

CHAPTER 50
DELIA

The earth shook and a beam of light shot from the Keystone. Delia could feel it burning the edges of her skin.

She resisted it – this new energy, unfamiliar and intense as it was. Next to her, Marjie was practically overflowing with bubbling watery energy, as if she'd become a stream herself. Agatha was lifted off the ground by an enormous gust of wind, while Ingrid stood strong and tall, like a great tree in the forest, as if connected with the earth itself.

Delia took a deep breath as the light continued to pierce into her chest. She knew she couldn't resist much longer. She knew it in her bones and blood. This was her fate. She needed to face her fear and embrace it.

"Drop your barriers," Marjie whispered.

And that was the exact right thing for Delia to hear at that moment.

She slowly exhaled the breath she'd been holding, allowing her shoulders to loosen, and then breathed in again, inhaling the energy of fire and welcoming it into her very being.

It no longer burned her; instead, it invigorated her in a way she'd never felt before.

She was passion in human form: inspiration, initiation.

She was the spark of new beginnings and the courage to carry on, the flames burning deep into the night of the campfire of all of humanity; creativity, protection, and drive.

She threw back her head and cackled, embracing the invigorating energy of the fire, becoming one with it. She was no longer afraid of the destructive danger, she was infatuated with all its other glorious potential.

"Now," said Ingrid, "it's time to combine our powers and connect with the stone."

The ground shook again. Delia couldn't help glancing around as she steadied herself against Marjie's and Agatha's hands that still gripped her own.

The Order had begun to advance, coming up against the barrier.

Some even looked like they had tried rolling in the mud to get through, but they could not.

"As soon as our powers are properly unleashed, there's a chance the shield shatters. And then we have to face them," Agatha muttered through a gale of wind.

"I'd say there's a high chance," said Ingrid.

"Can we delay it?" Delia asked. "I'm not sure I've quite got mastery of it yet. Give us a few months to practice and then I might be ready to fight that army."

Marjie chortled. "You'll be fine, dear. Can't you feel it? The power surging through us is truly magnificent."

"I do feel rather high," said Delia. "But that's not always the best time for making decisions. Ingrid should know that."

"The power of the dragons is ours!" Jerry boomed in a voice that reverberated through the dome of the shield still surrounding the stone.

"Dragons?!" said Ingrid. "If they managed to summon one, we'll have to destroy it quickly. We can't give them the upper hand."

"No," said Marjie. "Dragons are so endangered everyone thought they were extinct. We can't go murdering innocent creatures."

Agatha shook her head. "They're not innocent if the Order's corrupted them and is using them to manipulate, destroy, and take over the world."

"Still doesn't feel right," Marjie responded.

"I agree with Marjie," said Delia.

Ingrid furrowed her brow. "We have no choice."

"Unleash the beast!" the loud authoritarian voice commanded.

There was a thudding on the ground, so loud and heavy that

Delia could feel it rhythmically, like a great drum, through the swamp.

From the distance, an enormous creature approached.

The light given off by the Crones' combined powers and the Order's torches revealed a hairy, slimy, growling beast unlike anything she had ever seen or imagined.

"That's a dragon?" she asked. "I thought it would be more reptilian and less like an enormous canine monster."

The other Crones followed her gaze.

"That's no dragon," said Ingrid. "It's some kind of dog beast."

Just then, an orb of light appeared between them.

"This is it!" said Ingrid, bracing herself. "We are about to release the full power of the stone. Send your magic into it. Focus on the energy of the Crones. If that beast gives them the upper hand, dragon or not, we can't let them take over."

Delia felt her terror rising yet again. "But if we shatter the shield, we'll have no protection from it."

"Something tells me a beast like that could shatter the shield all on its own," said Agatha. "There's no time. We need to get this to work. We need all the power we can get."

This rang true for Delia. She joined the other Crones, pouring her fiery energy into the orb in front of them, connecting with the ancient power of the Crones and the old ones, whoever they were. As terrifying as they sounded, she'd rather they be on their side than against them.

The orb filled with the elements of fire, earth, air, and water, becoming larger and heavier as it sank down towards the stone, which began to melt into a kind of lava.

"Might want to take a step back," said Ingrid.

There was no time.

The stone shattered with a force so great that it hurled them all onto their backs.

Delia, only slightly winded, tried to regain her breath. She scrambled upwards to see that the stone itself had opened, breaking into large pieces.

A giant claw emerged from the ground, followed by another, and another.

A long, scaly, green arm began to protrude.

With a roar of flames, a dragon the size of a large elephant pushed its way out from deep within the earth.

"Now *that's* a dragon!" cried Ingrid, her eyes as big as saucers.

They all beheld the ancient creature in awe.

"Now, what was it that you said we were supposed to do with dragons?" Delia asked.

"It's beautiful," said Marjie. "What a majestic creature. Not going to kill it, are you?"

"Of course!" said Agatha. "A beast like that cannot be controlled."

Ingrid hesitated. "I've changed my mind," she said. "Our information was mixed up. Clearly." She shot Agatha a look.

"Hey, it's not my fault," Agatha protested. "I didn't write the books."

"The Dragons are part of the ancient power of the Crones," said Ingrid. "Figures! We should have known this."

"And what's that beast out there?" Delia asked.

"The Dragon's natural enemy," Ingrid replied. "I've heard a legend about this – the dog was cursed by a dragon and grew into a monster."

Delia felt a pang of sympathy towards the beast that was quickly overwhelmed by terror, but something didn't make sense.

"So why did the Order say they have the power of the Dragons?" Delia shouted as the dragon surveyed them, its enormous reptilian eyes swivelling between the four of them.

"They didn't," said Agatha. "They just said something about unleashing the dragon power. I suspect this is exactly what they're trying to control. Control the dragons and you control the world. But jokes on them. Dragons are clearly uncontrollable. Look at that intelligence! That regal majesty! That potency!"

"Let's talk about all this later," said Ingrid. "This is my dragon, and I need to connect with it."

"Why do you get all the fun?" Agatha grumbled.

"This is the Earth Dragon, obviously," said Ingrid. "Can't you feel it?"

Delia looked from the dragon to Ingrid. They did seem to have some kind of rapport, based on the way the ancient and wise creature was staring at the old forest witch.

"Go on then," said Marjie. "We haven't got all day."

The dome around them was indeed beginning to crack, and the ancient powers that held it seemed more unstable than ever as the enormous beast of the Order approached.

"Agatha's right," said Ingrid, climbing up towards the creature. "The Order wants the power of the dragons, and that's what they meant when they said the power of the Dragons is theirs." She stroked the emerald scales of the earth dragon. "Aren't you precious."

Delia's jaw dropped open. She'd never seen Ingrid show any particular kind of affection to any creature before, but apparently, the dragon had made her go all gooey.

There was a cracking noise, and the dome began to shatter around them.

"It's time," said Ingrid. "Let's show those boys who's boss. I'll teach them for trying to steal something that's not theirs. Fly, my pretty!"

The dragon roared and emerged, shaking its wings, lifted off the ground to the sky, and fire billowed from its mouth as it majestically and gracefully rose.

"I command you! Submit or perish!" cried Jerry's voice.

Delia giggled. She could sense the weakness in his tone, the slight tremble.

No one was going to mess with this dragon, not even that big scary dog.

The dome cracked under the pressure of the dragon's magic, as it rose up through the sky, the shield shattered into sparkles of magic.

The great dog barked and then whined a little.

"Attack!" cried Jerry's voice, and the troops began to march on the Crones, while the Beithíoch growled at the flying majestic reptile.

The four crones banded together back to back. "On three, we blast them to oblivion," said Ingrid.

"Right," Delia agreed, feeling much more confident, somehow, in her ability to use her power.

"The four of us together are far stronger than we are alone," said Marjie. "We've got this."

CHAPTER 51
THE CLERIC

The swamp was a mire of chaos and tension as the Order of Crimson advanced, surrounding their great beast. Ready for battle.

Every step they took seemed to reverberate through the murky terrain, sending ripples of unease through the Cleric's chest. His black boots sank into the damp earth, the sensation of each footfall weighing heavily on his soul.

Father Benedict, who he'd once revered as a leader, strode confidently ahead, his presence a stark contrast to the Cleric's own internal turmoil.

Jeremiah Benedict – for the Cleric now refused to use a title when he thought of the man – had been exposed as a hypocrite, his secret dalliances with women a stain on his supposed devotion to the Order's sacred mission.

The Cleric had fought himself for hours, but he simply couldn't deny the betrayal. He had feared admired and distained Benedict in equal measure, and now only the latter remained. The Shepherd's fall from grace within the Cleric's mind shook his very foundations.

It was not just Benedict's moral transgressions that gnawed at the Cleric's conscience. He harboured a deep suspicion that the man had also unwittingly betrayed the Order, whether through pride, arrogance, or some hidden agenda.

The Cleric's faith was shattered, replaced by a storm of doubt and distrust.

The air was thick with tension as the Order pressed forward, their determination evident in their resolute strides. The swamp seemed to close in around them, oppressive and suffocating, mirroring the oppressive weight on the Cleric's chest.

The beast's footfalls were like thunder.

The Order's most closely guarded secret was not a spell, a relic, nor a prophecy, but a creature of legend and might. The tale began when the last known dragon met its demise on English soil, felled by a gallant knight and his faithful hound. As the knight returned to the cheering crowds, the dragon's lethal poison, unbeknownst to all, had seeped into his battle-worn armour. While the townspeople celebrated, the knight's loyal dog, attempting to comfort and heal its master, licked the poisoned residue. Whispers spread that the loyal canine had succumbed to the venom, but the reality was far more astonishing.

As the dog lay, whimpering, a transformation of profound magnitude began. It swelled, growing in both stature and menace. Its once-gentle eyes now gleamed with an intelligence and fury that spoke of ancient powers and timeless grudges. The creature, having evolved into an entity both awe-inspiring and fearsome, had become an immortal embodiment of raw power.

Unbeknownst to all, members of the Order had observed this change, recognising the potential of this creature. Swiftly, they intervened, spiriting the new beast away under the cover of night and leaving behind the carcass of a stray to divert any suspicion.

Named 'Beithíoch' by the Order, but often merely called 'the beast', the creature's strength and fury only intensified over the years.

For the Order, the dragons were not merely to be hunted; they were the key to unparalleled power. Gaining control over a living dragon would mean not only controlling its immense power but also creating an army of Beithíoch warriors. For in achieving both, they would be invincible, and the fate of The Mission would be secured.

As they approached the shimmering barrier, the Cleric couldn't tear his gaze away from Father Benedict. The man who had once been his role model now appeared as a false shepherd, leading the flock astray.

The tension in the air grew unbearable.

The ground trembled beneath their feet, and the Cleric watched as the Order members attempted to breach the barrier, their efforts met with stubborn resistance. Some grew desperate, even rolling in the mud in a futile bid to pass through, but the barrier held fast.

The Cleric's heart pounded in his chest as he grappled with his internal conflict. Doubt and suspicion warred in his mind. As the Order's soldiers struggled against the unseen force before them, the swamp seemed to pulse with malevolent energy, as if it were a living entity, bearing witness to their internal strife.

The Crone power swelled.

All this had been orchestrated by Father Benedict, but at what cost?

The air crackled with energy as a sense of impending doom settled over the swamp. The tension escalated, and the Cleric watched in growing horror as the very ground beneath them began to quake.

It was as if the swamp itself had come alive, responding to forces beyond their comprehension. The swamp's ancient secrets, long buried beneath layers of muck and darkness, were now stirring, and the Cleric couldn't help but feel that they had awakened something they could never hope to control.

And then, the very thing the Order had been waiting centuries for finally happened. From the heart of the swamp, from the stone they had long believed to be a source of power, emerged a creature beyond their wildest nightmares. A real-life dragon, majestic and fearsome, rose from the depths of the earth, blowing the Crones back.

The Cleric's heart pounded in his chest as he watched the

monstrous being, its scales glistening with an otherworldly sheen. But there was no doubt in his mind; this creature could not be anything but evil.

It was a manifestation of the corruption that had taken hold of the Shepherd.

"Begin the ritual," Father Benedict commanded, his eyes gleaming with malice, his voice resonant with a power that was more diabolical than divine. The Cleric watched as the Order's most powerful mages stepped forward, drawing a circle of power in the dark soil of the swamp. They began their incantations, voices rising in a cacophony of dark promise.

The Cleric's mind raced. This was not the Order's way – the way of purity and righteousness. This was ambition, raw and unbridled. The Shepherd was not the selfless leader he portrayed; he was corrupt, his soul tainted by the very power he sought to control.

The dragon was in the air now, but soon it would be chained and drugged with magic – the majestic beast of legend.

A wave of mist rushed into the sky, propelled by the Order's mages. The dragon roared, a sound of fury and anguish, and the Cleric felt a pang of sympathy. Perhaps this creature was not the enemy; it was a mere pawn in the Shepherd's game.

He watched as the Essence of Dominion was brought forth, a relic of ancient times, pulsing with a light pierced through the gloom of the swamp. The enormous hulking Beithíoch, ever obedient to its master's will, lumbered towards the dragon.

The two great beasts collided in a cacophony of growls that

rumbled the earth. The dragon had the upper hand, but for how long? The mages were preparing the next stage of their trap while the Crones sent waves of elemental magic at the pawn soldiers positioned before them, mere distractions from the real quest.

The Cleric looked upon Father Benedict and saw him for what he truly was: a man drunk on power, wielding the name of the Almighty for his own twisted ends.

In that moment, the Cleric knew that Benedict's betrayal ran deep, that he had been corrupted by the allure of power and had hatched a plan that could only lead to destruction. The dragon, he was certain, was a pawn in Benedict's scheme, a tool to seize the power they sought for his own arrogant purposes.

He could not stand idly by as the Order was led astray by the delusions of one man.

In a bold and unprecedented move, the Cleric made a decision that went against everything he had ever known. He backed away from the Shepherd, reached for the horn at his belt, held it to his mouth, and blew out the sound of retreat.

"Retreat. We must live to fight another day," he cried to the soldiers around him. Many of whom followed his orders at once. Even the mages stopped their magic.

"No! You fools!" Father Benedict cried. "Do not retreat!"

But his voice was drowned out by another roar from the dragon and the Cleric felt a sweet satisfaction. After all, Benedict wanted nothing more than to advance, destroying countless lives in the wake of his own pride.

The swamp, once a battleground, now seemed like a test of morals. As the Order began to scurry in confusion, the Cleric turned and began to move in the opposite direction.

His steps were resolute, and his heart heavy with the weight of his decision, and yet there was no other way.

CHAPTER 52
DELIA

Delia watched the chaos rise through swamp, her heart pounding as the Order guards continued to advance. She and the other Crones had been blown back away from the Keystone as the glorious dragon had emerged, but they'd quickly regrouped. She could hear the distant sounds of the Order's chants and the dragon's roars.

"Something's not right out there," Marjie said.

"It's probably just your blasted intuition again," Agatha grumbled.

"I vote in favour of Marjie's intuition," said Delia. "It saved my neck at the theatre, and besides, something tells me the Order have planned all of this out. Look – over there – they're doing something magical. I bet they've been after the dragon this whole time!"

"Blast it all!" said Ingrid. "You're probably right. But we're not going to stand idly by and let them take her."

Agatha cracked her knuckles. "Not on my watch." She raised her hands, sending a blast of focussed wind towards the nearest soldiers as Marjie, next to her, summoned a wave from the swamp puddles.

"These new powers are wicked!" Marjie cackled with glee.

Delia heard the sound of a horn in the distance, but rather than worrying what it meant, she focused her energy and sent a plume of fire outwards, sending Order soldiers scurrying away as Ingrid's magic made the ground come alive with roots and vines that grabbed at the Order minions, pulling them back.

The stone they stood around glowed with power, and Delia savoured the ancient strength flowing through her. It was wild and strong, the complete opposite of the Order's dark magic.

The Dragon was now ensnared in magical ropes, the great dog baying at her, and yet the Order was in chaos.

"Let's combine our power!" Marjie suggested.

"Alright, on the count of three. One, two, three!" Ingrid cried.

The crones raised their hands, and Delia felt a great furnace surging through her with such force that the Order members approaching, weaving strange spells in the air and holding ancient swords and bows, were blown back.

The ground surged up, like ripples in the water and mud of the swamp, covering the soldiers with mud. A great gale, like a tornado, blasted them back, and then fire singed their hair and clothing – a warning this time, at least.

Next time, Delia might not be so controlled.

She smiled a satisfied smile as the older members closest to them squealed and screamed and scampered back. Even their dog beast retreated in the face of the tremendous Crone power.

She thought she caught a glimpse of Jerry, singed right down to his underpants, running away like a little rabbit.

That made her giggle, which was apparently infectious, because moments later, all four of the Crones were rolling in the mud and laughing hysterically.

The dragon came to rest behind them, huffing out some steam from its nostrils in a way that reminded Delia of Ingrid. Delia wasn't sure if she was unimpressed, as the forest witch tended to be, or if she was just having a little rest. After all, that was a lot of exertion for a creature trapped in the earth for perhaps hundreds of years.

"I call that a success," said Marjie. "But I think it's time for some tea."

"That's for sure," Ingrid agreed.

"And some sherry," Agatha added hopefully.

Marjie cast a quick cleansing charm over all of them, making Delia feel a tingling fresh sensation as if she'd just stepped out of a good shower into clean clothes. "I really must learn that one," she muttered, looking at her friend in awe.

They began trudging through the swamp, back into the forest towards Agatha's hut.

The dragon, without any coaxing at all, followed on behind them, her heavy footsteps beating a steady drum into the earth.

Ingrid behaved as if this was the most normal thing in the world, while Delia kept turning her head back to catch a glimpse of the beautiful being if only to marvel in awe at the entire situation.

She wasn't afraid at all of the creature.

The earth dragon seemed old, beyond words, and with wisdom to match.

She wasn't a pet, and could never be anything so diminutive, but her magic was somehow linked with the Crones in general and with Ingrid in particular.

If Delia wasn't so in awe, she'd be green with envy. "Imagine having your own dragon," she muttered.

"Perhaps we all do," said Marjie. "After all, there are four of us. There are four elements. Why wouldn't there be four dragons?"

"I don't know about that," said Ingrid. "I've heard dragons were hunted to extinction. What are the chances there are four?"

"Do you think all dragons are elemental?" Delia asked.

"Who knows?" said Agatha. "They're ancient creatures. It's a bit like asking about the dinosaurs. Nobody has any clue. They just pretend they're all scaly when actually it's possible they had feathers according to more recent theories."

"It makes them seem less like big scary lizards. More like giant Muppets," Delia said, but nobody laughed at her joke. Perhaps none of them had ever been exposed to the children's show, given that none of them, as far as she knew, had any children of their own. She wasn't about to start asking questions.

They continued on through the forest, on a surprisingly smooth path, no doubt aided by Ingrid's magic, or perhaps by the dragon. Delia was too tired to ask. The trees seemed to move out of the way for them, and the earth rolled out like a carpet, soft but not too muddy underneath.

It was magical and dreamlike. Delia almost felt as if she were drifting along.

Before long the hut appeared before them; the lights were on, shining warmly through the windows.

They burst into the warm, cosy atmosphere. Stew was bubbling on the stove, and Delia found herself even more in awe of the forest witch than she had been before.

It's one thing to get a teapot to float across the room. It's quite another to somehow have a wholesome dinner cooked and ready when you get home, without even having a crockpot.

She added it to the list of mysteries that she would one day feel comfortable asking Ingrid about, but today was not a day for any more activity.

Ingrid tended to the dragon in the back garden while the other Crones made themselves at home.

Delia yawned and gravitated towards her window seat. She pulled a blanket over her legs, sipped her relaxing tea, and ate two bowls of stew before drifting off to sleep, the sound of an owl hooting outside, the fire crackling, and just a little bit of snoring from Agatha, until Marjie stopped it with a very cunning and enviable charm.

One day, Delia thought to herself, *I'm going to be able to do more than just set things on fire. I'm going to have to do something useful. Magical housework, that's the real fantasy.*

She woke with the dawn breaking, a pale light on the horizon.

Ingrid was sitting at the kitchen table, grinding herbs in a mortar and pestle. It was that gritty sound that must have woken Delia from her dreams.

...dreams of flame that had somehow been more peaceful than her usual nightmares.

There were still so many mysteries left unsolved, especially about Delia's own family, and her mind started to think over them.

"Stop that," said Agatha, staring at her sternly from an armchair.

"What?" Delia asked.

Agatha squinted at her. "You're going in circles in your brain. I can almost hear it from here."

"Are you actually psychic now?" Delia asked.

"I'm not psychic," Agatha grumbled. "I can just tell you're thinking too much."

"Maybe," Delia admitted. "There is a faint buzzing in my head."

Agatha shrugged. "Maybe I am also thinking too much. It takes one to know one."

Marjie cooked a fabulous breakfast from supplies she'd somehow stashed in her rather small handbag.

"I'm not sure about all this modern food," said Ingrid,

stuffing another pancake into her mouth followed by another scone.

Marjie and Delia made eye contact and giggled.

"So, you're going to stick around, then?" said Agatha, looking pointedly at Delia.

"I'm not sure if I want to return to London after my last performance," said Delia. "Besides, I've already rented a house. All my friends are here. Even Kitty, for now, at least. And Gillian's not far away and the children are coming to stay with me for a while, provided it's safe enough now."

"That's just lovely, dear," said Marjie. "We're so pleased to have you around. I do believe you might find that Myrtlewood is more of a home than you've ever known before."

Delia smiled. "You know, I think you might be right."

EPILOGUE

The Cleric's footsteps echoed in the hollow silence as he approached the high tower of the Order where the Elders met, his heart a battleground of conviction and apprehension. His mind was set; he would expose Father Benedict, the Crimson Shepherd, and expose the rot at his core. Surely, the Cleric would be exalted, perhaps even earning the title of Crimson Shepherd for himself. But the reality he faced was starkly different from the justice he envisioned.

Father Benedict, standing tall and unyielding, met the Cleric's gaze with a steely look that sent shivers down his spine. The Elders stood behind him, staring disdainfully towards the Cleric as he blustered and pointed and accused Benedict of all manner of corruption.

"You return to us with accusations, but it is you who will face judgment," the Shepherd declared, his voice resonating with a confidence that seemed to draw from an unseen well of authority.

The Cleric's protests died in his throat as he realised the tables had turned back before he'd even had a chance to topple them. Benedict's claim – that every deed he'd carried out, no matter how vile, was in service of the Almighty's will – was unshakable, and the Cleric's doubts were now a heresy against their divine mission.

As guards seized him, the Cleric felt the weight of his failed coup. He was dragged through the labyrinth of the compound, the murmurs of his once-peers now a scornful chorus marking his disgrace.

Finally, they reached an iron door, the sight of which was chilling. Blindfolds were tied firmly around the eyes of the guards that held him before they entered.

The door opened to reveal an austere chamber. The only thing in sight was a small square iron door set into the centre of the wall, adorned in intricate sigils.

The Cleric was positioned in front of this and the air grew heavy with dread as the small iron door creaked open.

The Cleric's imagination conjured up images of divine brilliance, a radiant being that would strike him with awe and compel him to his knees in repentance. But what awaited him was far from divine.

And in that moment, the Cleric realised at once what had driven Father Benedict mad with power.

Terror gripped the Cleric, along with the realisation that the

Almighty he had served, the god he had envisioned, was a dark terror, so ominous his eyes could barely take in any aspect.

It was an abyss, a malevolent darkness filled with whispers that clawed at his sanity as his eyes met not with the light of salvation but a void so profound it seemed to devour the very essence of his being.

The moonlight bathed the temple in a serene, silver glow as Mathilda made her way to the inner sanctum, her heart heavy with anticipation. The air was thick with the scent of night blooms and sacred incense, and the soft murmur of the Clochar's nocturnal life whispered through the corridors. She had been summoned urgently by her elders, and the gravity of their request weighed on her.

As she entered the sanctum, the elder sisters, Gwyneth and Franwen, awaited her, their faces etched with both excitement and solemnity. The room was dimly lit, the flickering candles casting long, dancing shadows against the stone walls.

"Mathilda," Gwyneth began, her voice steady but laced with urgency, "the time we have long anticipated is upon us. The Crone magic, it's awakening."

Mathilda's breath caught in her throat. She had felt the stirrings, the subtle shifts in the air, but to hear it spoken aloud made it all the more real.

Franwen stepped forward, her fiery red hair seeming to

absorb the candlelight. "We must act swiftly. The power of the Crones is a force unlike any other. If harnessed, it could change everything for the Sisterhood. It belongs here, rightfully."

Mathilda felt a surge of apprehension. "I understand the power belongs to the sisterhood," she said, her voice a mere whisper. "But my sister is so stubborn, and now she and her friends will be even more powerful."

Franwen's eyes met Mathilda's, a spark of determination in their depths. "We have been preparing for this moment, Mathilda. The prophecies, the ancient texts, all point to this time. You must act swiftly."

"Why me?" Mathilda asks.

"Ingrid is your sister," said Gwyneth simply.

"But she's your..." Mathilda started but stopped as sister Gwyneth's eyes darted to the floor.

Franwen cut in. "Your connection with Ingrid can be leveraged. She will help you, even if she never listens to anyone."

Mathilda felt a weight settle deeper upon her shoulders, a daunting burden.

"But what of the balance?" Mathilda questioned, her mind racing with the implications. "The Crones' power is part of a greater whole. To disrupt it could have consequences we cannot foresee."

Gwyneth stepped closer, her presence commanding yet reassuring. "We understand the risks, but the rewards, Mathilda, are beyond measure. This is about more than power; it's about restoration, about bringing back a divine harmony long lost."

Franwen's gaze was intense, piercing. "The world is changing, Mathilda. We must change with it, adapt, grow stronger. The Crones' magic is the key."

"I will do it," Mathilda said, her voice firm. "I will reach out to Ingrid. But we must tread carefully. She's not easily fooled."

Sabrina Bracewell sat alone in the grand drawing room of the Bracewell-Thorn mansion, the flickering flames of the fireplace casting dancing shadows across the room as she sipped the last of her artemisia tea.

The fire crackled and popped, a comforting yet eerie soundtrack to her brooding. Sabrina's eyes, sharp and calculating, reflected the flames as she contemplated the recent events. The family records in Myrtlewood had been accessed, a violation of the highest order, and by none other than that interloper, Delia Spark. The very thought of it made her blood boil.

As she stared into the fire, Sabrina felt a surprise surge of power course through her veins. It was an ancient, primal force, one that she had long awaited but never truly expected to feel. The Crone power belonging to the Bracewell line was awakening. Her heart quickened. This was her destiny.

The fire flared suddenly, casting a bright glow across the room. Sabrina's eyes gleamed with a new intensity. The power of the fire crone was within her grasp, a force so potent and so deeply connected to her lineage.

But there was an obstacle, a thorn in her side – Delia Spark. That woman, with her audacious claim to the Bracewell legacy, was a pretender, an impostor.

Sabrina knew that Delia must be dealt with, and swiftly. The power of the fire crone was not to be shared, especially not with someone as unworthy as Delia.

Sabrina rose from her chair, her movements graceful yet filled with a newfound purpose. The fire continued to crackle behind her, a symbol of the power she was about to claim. Her birthright.

A personal message from Iris

Hello my lovelies! Thank you so much for joining me and the Myrtlewood Crones. If you enjoyed this book, please leave a rating or review to help other people find it!

If you're ready to read more, you can order the third Myrtlewood Crones book, Crone of Elders Blaze.

If this is your first time reading my books, you might also want to check out the original Myrtlewood Mysteries series, starting with Accidental Magic.

If you're looking for more books set in the same world, you might want to take a look at my Dreamrealm Mysteries series too.

I absolutely love writing these books and sharing them with

you. Feel free to join my reader list and follow me on social media to keep up to date with my witchy adventures.

Many blessings,

Iris xx

P.S. You can also subscribe to my Patreon account for extra Myrtlewood stories and new chapters of my books before they're published, as well as real magical content like meditations and spells, and access to my Myrtlewood Discord community. Subscribing supports my writing and other creative work!

For more information, see: www.patreon.com/IrisBeagle hole

About the Author

Iris Beaglehole

Iris Beaglehole is many peculiar things, a writer, researcher, analyst, druid, witch, parent, and would-be astrologer. She loves tea, cats, herbs, and writing quirky characters.

facebook.com/IrisBeaglehole

x.com/IrisBeaglehole

instagram.com/irisbeaglehole

Printed in Great Britain
by Amazon